Making Money With PVC Pipe Furniture

Including "Making Money With Stained Glass"

Sam Glassman

Lion

This publication is designed to provide accurate and authoritative information in regard to the subject matter covered. It is sold with the understanding that the publisher is not engaged in rendering legal, accounting, or other professional service. If legal advice or other expert assistance is required, the services of a competent professional should be sought.

Copyright © 1986 by Lion Publishing Company. All rights reserved. Printed in the United States of America. No part of this book may be used or reproduced in any manner whatsoever without written permission except in the case of brief quotations embodied in critical articles or reviews.

For information, write
P.O. Box 151034, San Diego, CA 92115.

Bendah, David
Making Money With PVC Pipe Furniture.
Library of Congress Catalog Card No. 85-090841

ISBN 0-933301-13-8

Table of Contents

Introduction 7
Explanation 10
Patio Chairs 15
Bar Accessories 20
Indoor Chairs 25
Tables 30
Glider Chairs 37
Miscellaneous Accessories 42
Making Money With Stained Glass 47
Ordering PVC Materials 60

Introduction

Unlike most crafts, making PVC furniture requires a minimum of skill — and the result is furniture that looks good, is inexpensive to make, and will not corrode, rust, chip or peel. In addition, a wide range of durable equipment — pick-up truck side rails, swing sets, sandbox covers — can be easily fashioned from PVC tubing.

PVC, or polyvinyl chloride, is one of the most versatile man-made synthetic resins — it's hard, chemical-resistant, and impervious to the sun's ultra-violet rays. It is used in products ranging from fabrics and floor coverings to both indoor and outdoor plumbing pipes. These qualities make it ideal for furniture and equipment that must be both attractive and rugged.

PVC Details You Need To Know, Tools You Need To Have

As you progress into more complicated structures, you will eventually need all of the following simple hand tools:

- Sawhorses or workbench
- Hand saw or hack saw
- Measuring tape, at least 6 feet
- Sandpaper, rough and smooth grade
- Pencil
- Small hand or electric drill with bits
- Miter box
- Screwdriver
- Plastic pipe cement for gluing pipes together

You can buy PVC pipe made especially for furniture — it has a high gloss which permeates the pipe walls and is very tough, stronger even than PVC pipe made for plumbing. Pipe made especially for furniture costs more, but the quality and appearance make the final design worth the extra expense. There are other advantages: you buy it free of scuffs and manufacturers' markings, so you don't have to clean it. The fittings have beveled ends. Special joints are manufactured for furniture, so more design options are open to you.

Furniture-grade PVC pipe costs more than the regular variety pipe, but it's really worth the few dollars more. Your furniture will be more durable. You can purchase all your materials at reasonable prices from:

Available Plastics, Inc.
P.O. Box 924
Huntsville, Alabama 35804
205-859-4957

The PVC pipe normally used is SCH 40, or Schedule 40, in 1¼, 1½ and 2-inch diameters. Most of the designs in this book call for 1½" pipe. Other than the pipe lengths, you will need PVC fittings to connect the pipes; these fittings are:

- Connectors
- Crosses, such as the 3-way, 4-way or 5-way slip cross
- Reduction fittings which connect the ends of different-size pipes
- Tees
- 45-degree ells, or elbows
- Right-angle (90-degree) ells
- Street ell, which has a male fitting at one end, female at the other. Also called 90-degree slip elbow
- Street elbow, set at 45 degrees with a male fitting at one end, female at the other; also called 45-degree slip elbow

- 3-way ells
- Ys
- End, or slip, cap

Cleaning PVC Pipe

Furniture-grade pipe should be free of marks, but plumbing grade pipe will probably have to be cleaned. It's simple. The first step is to clean off the manufacturer's marks that run the length of the pipes. Household soap pads do the job, but not easily; instead, soak 00 steel wool in lacquer thinner or commercial acetone. With firm rubbing, the manufacturer's marks and shipping scuffs come off easily. As you move down the length of the pipe, clean off the rubbed area with a clean cloth. This method works equally well for removing plastic pipe cement that oozes from joints.

Painting

Painting PVC pipe furniture is easy. Simply clean the piece with fine sandpaper or wipe with acetone. You can use a paint brush, but a spray can is easier and does a better job. Use any good plastic-base paint. Lacquer-base paint attacks PVC like acid.

Often, painting is unnecessary because PVC pipe comes in many colors; however, if you do want to paint the pipes, you'll find PVC pipe made especially for furniture is tough to work with because of its hard finish. Pipe from the hardware store has a softer finish.

Woodgraining

Woodgrained PVC pipe, with practice, can look like wood — almost. You're not going to fool anyone, but it's an interesting effect. Always wear safety glasses. Attach a heavy-guage wire wheel to an electric drill or bench grinder, and either:

- Brace the drill and move the PVC pipe lengthways along the wheel; or
- Brace the PVC pipe and move the drill and wheel lengthways along it.

Clean the pipe by wiping it with a soft, clean cloth. After the pipe is clean and free from any dirt and scuff marks, it's ready to be painted or stained. This isn't as easy as it sounds — it takes practice, so try it out on scraps first.

Cutting PVC Pipe

Since PVC is rigid plastic, you can cut it by using just about any kind of saw. But it's best to use a carbide saw blade; hacksaws are sometimes difficult to handle. Also, hand-held hacksaws are time-consuming and you can't always get a straight line. It would be worth the extra expense of purchasing an inexpensive Miter box. Be sure you don't cut on a slant. You'll find sawing PVC pipe a lot like sawing wood, only much easier.

To spare yourself a lot of small and wasteful scrap pieces at the end, remember to cut the longest pieces first. As you cut a pipe, mark on it its length, number, and letter with yellow pencil. In this way, group together all pipes of the same length.

Assembling PVC Pipe

After you have cut all the lengths of pipe and have the various joints, or pipe connectors, assemble the project according to the appropriate plan. Do not glue anything together yet. The idea is to assemble the project once or twice before cementing, so you have practice, know what you're doing, and are comfortable with it. Try to visualize at least two steps ahead as you assemble so you know what your next move will be.

When the unglued project is assembled, check to see that it's all square and that the sides are all even. When you are satisfied with the assembling, be sure to mark with a yellow pencil a line across the connectors and pipes. This is an important step because when you glue, it'll be easier to see that the connectors are facing the correct way — you won't put any pieces on backward.

So, before you glue anything, you must have:

1. Cut all the correct lengths, marked the correct length and number
2. Made sure you have all the connectors
3. Assembled the project in at least one dry run
4. Marked the connectors and pipe with yellow pencil
5. Read and understood the safety directions on the cement can: avoid breathing the fumes as much as possible; don't get any cement on your skin; work outside or in a well-ventilated room.

Gluing PVC Pipe

Gluing PVC pipe is fairly easy. But it's also easy to make a costly mistake. That's why it's so important to assemble and mark which pieces go where before you begin to glue.

It's also important to use the right kind of glue. Clear PVC cement will produce the best results. The cement should be either medium or heavy bodied. The thinner light-bodied cement is not as durable.

Working on a workbench or some kind of level surface, do just one small section at a time. Take a section of your unglued project, take apart one piece and glue it. Put the glue in the fitting and just a small amount around the end of the pipe. This lubricates both pieces so that they will fit easily. The cement dries quickly, so there's not much time to maneuver. Do not overdo it with the glue; if there's too much, it will ooze out of the fittings and make the final clean-up more difficult.

If cement does ooze out, simply wipe it off with a facial tissue or paper towel. Try to do this while the cement is still wet — it's difficult to remove after it has hardened.

To ensure a tight fit, twist the pipe slightly so that the yellow pencil mark on the fitting lines up exactly with the yellow pencil mark on the pipe; then give the pipe one last push into the fitting to make sure it is firmly in. If there is any resistance, use a rubber mallot and gently hammer the piece into the other piece.

Continue piece by piece until the project is complete — unless you are working on a project with slings to support cushions. If so, leave one side unglued to the main structure and attach it with metal screws so you will be able to put on and remove the slings. See the individual plans for more details.

Should you glue a fitting incorrectly, saw off the pipe at the point it enters the fitting; keep the now too-short pipe for another project. With a hacksaw blade, cut through the section of pipe still in the fitting, making sure you don't cut into the fitting itself. Then, push a screwdriver between the section of pipe and the fitting and the pipe will come out.

Seats and Cushions

Almost any kind of normal cushion material is fine, such as the many types of vinyl, Herculite, or canvass. But choose a material appropriate for the piece and its location. Herculite and canvass are best for outdoor use. Denim, corduroy and other durable materials are good for indoor use.

Plans for the various seats are found later in the book, so consider this just general information. Following those patterns, sew three sides together, double stitching every seam; some materials will pull apart if you don't turn the edge under before sewing to make it double-strength. Leave an open edge in one side of the cushion — this is where you'll be inserting the polyurethane foam stuffing.

If you can't sew, pay someone piece-work to make your cushions — it won't be costly. Or, buy cushions ready-made on sale at inexpensive stores.

Experimenting with PVC

After working with PVC, you may want to experiment with the different designs. PVC pipe becomes soft when heated and hard when cooled, which means you can do a variety of designs when you heat up the pipe. Heating the pipe is simple: preheat your oven to 250 degrees Fahrenheit. Put the pipe on an oven-proof pan and leave it in the oven for a minute — no more. Be careful pulling the pipe out of the oven — it may be hot. Quickly insert a dry elbow. A dry elbow is a form you may purchase from a hardware store or from a PVC supplier. The dry elbow is used to mold or bend the PVC pipe into a circular or arc shape. When you get the desired shape, immerse the pipe in cold water.

Safety

Although PVC is one of the easiest furniture materials to work with, attention to safety is still a must. Saws are sharp, no matter what you're cutting.

Always follow safety instructions, such as those on the plastic cement can. Pay close attention to the cutting line, saw edges and drill bits, especially when using power tools.

Keep your work area clean and clear of clutter. A carelessly laid power tool or section of PVC pipe or is easy to trip over. In addition, a clean work space will make you more efficient and your task safer.

Saving Money

As an alternative to Schedule 40 PVC pipe, you can buy the cheaper 160-psi (pounds-per-square-inch) pipe; it has thinner walls and is much less rugged. It is useful to experiment with and for projects that don't have to take much stress.

Also, at construction and landscaping sites, small sections of PVC are often thrown away. Ask if you can have them. Or, ask plumbers for their waste pieces.

Now you're on your way to crafting durable furniture and equipment that you'll be proud to use. After you've created a few practice pieces, you'll be ready to craft PVC furniture to sell. PVC patio furniture is really popular right now, and it's less costly than redwood and more durable than plastic or metal patio furniture. Plus, you never have to paint it or protect it from inclement weather — PVC doesn't fade in the hot sun and it holds up well in freezing temperatures.

1
Patio Chairs

INSTRUCTIONS

It is preferable to assemble on a flat, padded surface.
All pipes must sit firmly in their sockets.
Refer often to the diagrams.

1. Lay Part "A" flat so that two open sockets point up.
2. Insert the pipe end of PART "C" into the socket on PART "A" that does not point up. The open socket on PART "C" should point up.
3. Insert a "B" PIPE into each flap loop of the SLING.
4. Position the SLING with the "B" PIPES over PART "A" and "C" so that the "B" PIPE in the shortest flap fits SOCKET 1, the "B" PIPE in the widest flap loop fits in SOCKET 3, and the other "B" PIPE fits in SOCKET 2. Connect. It will be necessary to stretch the SLING in order to make the connections.
5. Lay PART "D" flat so that two open sockets point up.
6. Insert the pipe end of PART "E" into the socket on PART "D" that does not point up. The open socket on PART "E" should point up.
7. Position PART "D" and "E" over the "B" PIPES so that the "B" PIPE in the shortest SLING flap fits SOCKET 4, the "B" PIPE in the widest SLING flap loop fits SOCKET 6, and the other "B" PIPE fits SOCKET 5. Connect.
8. There are 6 screws. Insert each into a screw hole indicated by small screws (▼) on Diagram 1. Fasten each.
9. Turn the chair frame right side up and place a cushion on the SLING. Enjoy!

SUPER LOUNGE CHAIR
LC 205

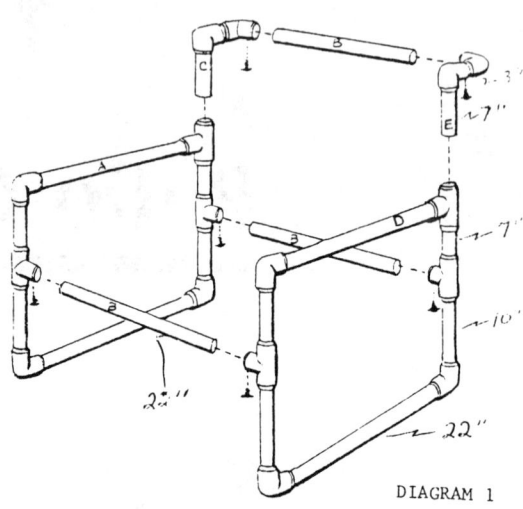
DIAGRAM 1

INVENTORY	
PART	QUANTITY
A	1
B	3
C	2
D	1
E	1
Sling	1
Cushion	1
Screws	6

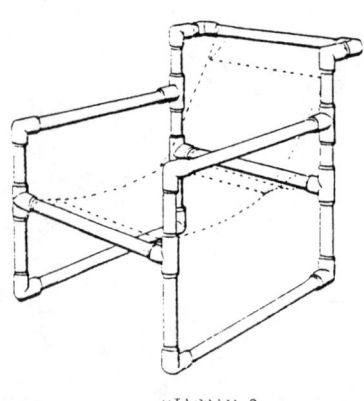

DIAGRAM 2

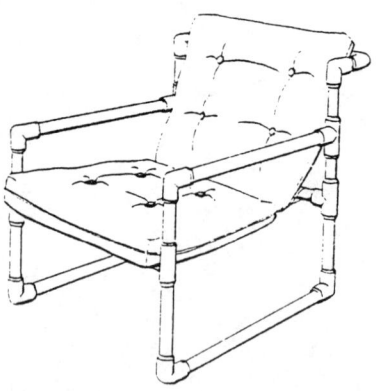
DIAGRAM 3

BASIC LOUNGE CHAIR
LC 101 / LC 201

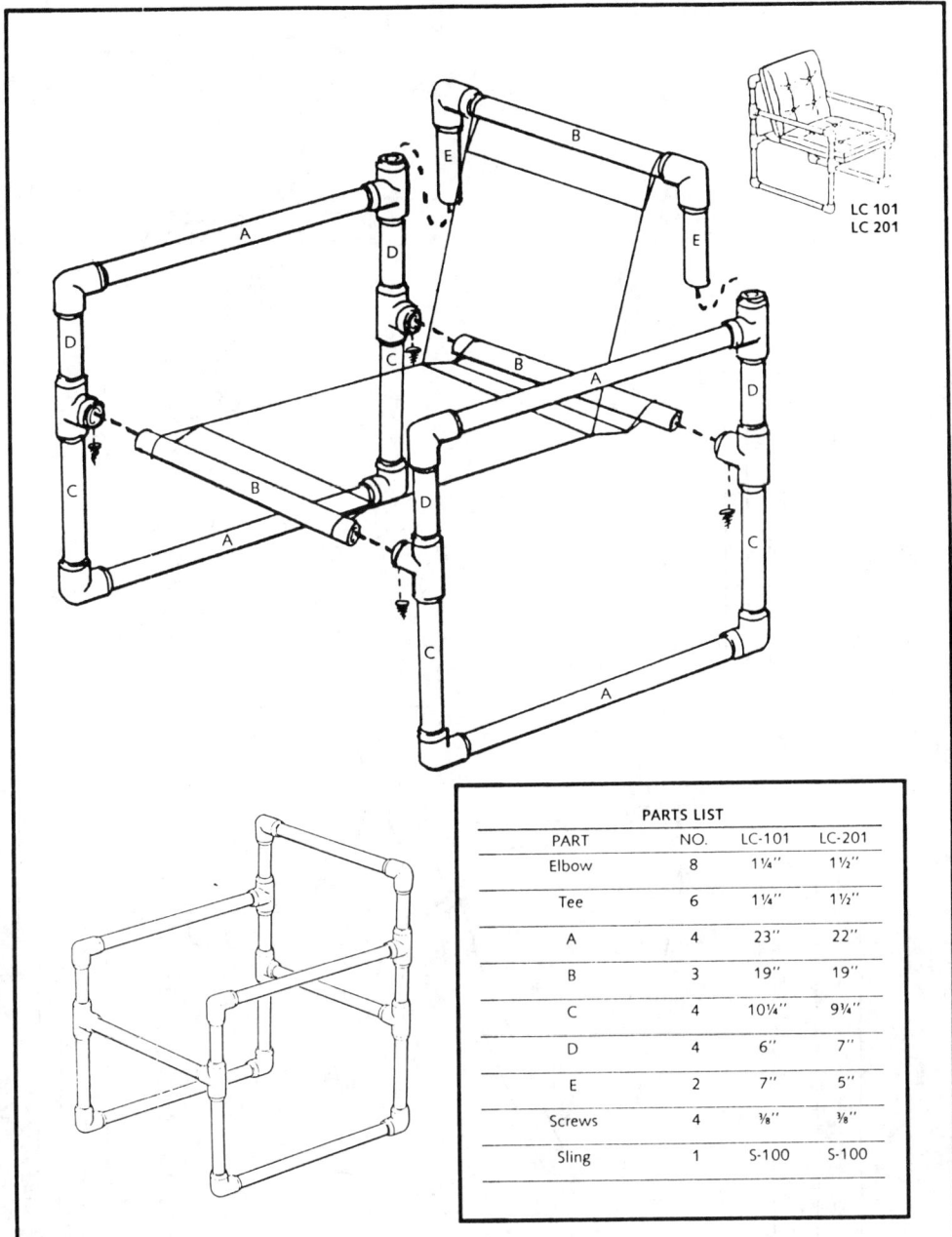

PARTS LIST			
PART	NO.	LC-101	LC-201
Elbow	8	1¼"	1½"
Tee	6	1¼"	1½"
A	4	23"	22"
B	3	19"	19"
C	4	10¼"	9¾"
D	4	6"	7"
E	2	7"	5"
Screws	4	⅜"	⅜"
Sling	1	S-100	S-100

CHAISE LOUNGE CL-101

PARTS LIST 1 1/4"

PART	SIZE	NO.
A	22"	2
B	19"	4
C	11 3/4"	10
D	2 3/8"	2
E	24" w/tee	2
F	18"	1

PARTS LIST 3/4" CTS

PART	SIZE	NO.
H	24½"	1
I	14 3/4"	2
J	14 3/4" slotted chaise mechanism	4
K	1½"	

FITTINGS PART LIST 1¼" and 3/4"

PART	SIZE	NO.
ELBOW	1¼"	12
TEE	1¼"	4
SLIP-T	1¼"	4
ELBOW	1¼"	2 w/ 7/8" hole
ELBOW	3/4"	4
TEE	3/4"	2

PARTS LIST		
Part	Size	No.
Elbow	1¼"	10
Tee	1¼"	6
A	24"	9
B	10"	4
C	4"	6
Sling	28" x 78"	1
Glue	¼ pt	1

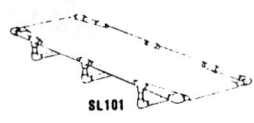

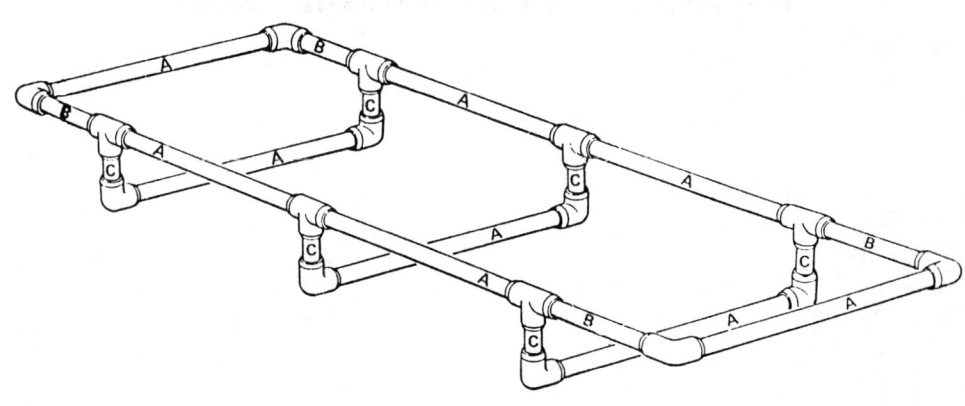

2

Bar Accessories

BAR STOOL
BS 103

INSTRUCTIONS

It is recommended that assembly be done on a padded surface.
All pipes must sit firmly in their sockets.
Refer often to the Diagrams.

1. Take PART "A" and lay it flat with open sockets facing up.
2. Take four "B" PIPES and insert the end of each into one of the four open sockets of PART "A".
3. Take PART "C" and connect two "B" PIPES so that PART "C" runs the same direction as the crosspipe in PART "A". Repeat.
4. Take four "B" PIPES and insert the end of each into one of the four open sockets on the two "C" PIPES.
5. Take a "D" PART and connect two "B" PIPES with the open sockets on the "D" PART. The "D" PART should be directly over a "C" PART. Repeat.
6. Examine a SLING. Insert an "E" PART through the SLING. Connect the facing ends of the "D" PARTS. Note that one end has a bent pipe attached to it. Make sure that the seam of the SLING is on the bottom.
7. Take an "E" PART. Insert it through the SLING so that the bent pipe end is directly acrosss from the bent pipe end of the other "E" PART. Fit one end of the "E" PART onto the pipe end of one of the "D" PARTS. Pull the other end, stretching the SLING, and fit it onto the remaining "D" PART pipe. The SLING should fit on the center pipe of the "E" PARTS.
8. Take the remaining SLING and stretch it over the bent pipes of the "E" PARTS. Slide it down until it is just above the fittings. Make sure that the seam of the SLING is toward the back.
9. Examine the "F" PART. Note that it curves. Fit the open sockets over the bent pipes of the "E" PARTS so that the curve extends out away from the center of the chair. This will be a tight fit. The bar stool is ready to enjoy!

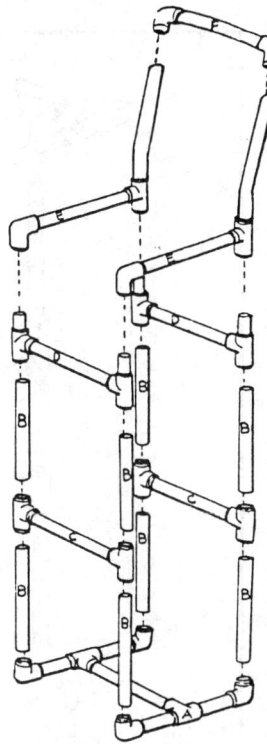

DIAGRAM 1

INVENTORY	
PART	QUANTITY
A	1
B	8
C	2
D	2
E	2
F	1
Slings	2

See Page 5E
Dining Chair   DC 102
for dimensions

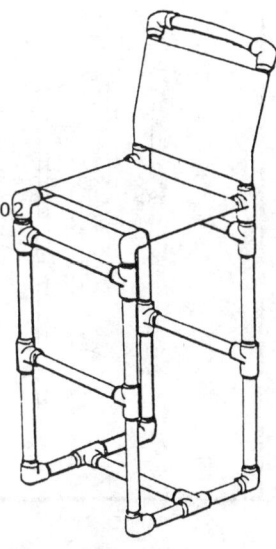

DIAGRAM 2

BAR
BR 102

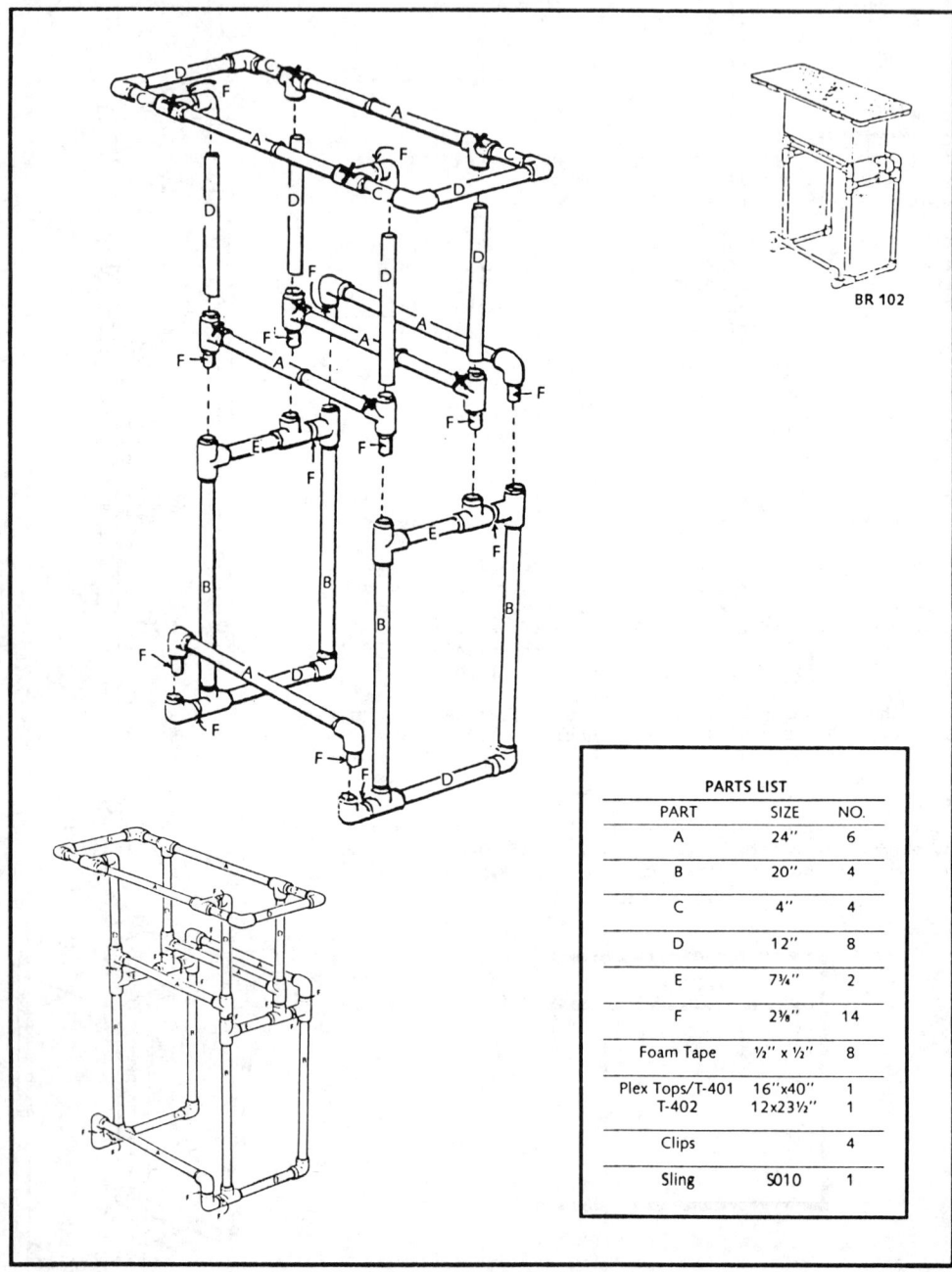

BR 102

PARTS LIST		
PART	SIZE	NO.
A	24"	6
B	20"	4
C	4"	4
D	12"	8
E	7¾"	2
F	2⅜"	14
Foam Tape	½" x ½"	8
Plex Tops/T-401	16"x40"	1
T-402	12x23½"	1
Clips		4
Sling	S010	1

BAR STOOL
BS 101

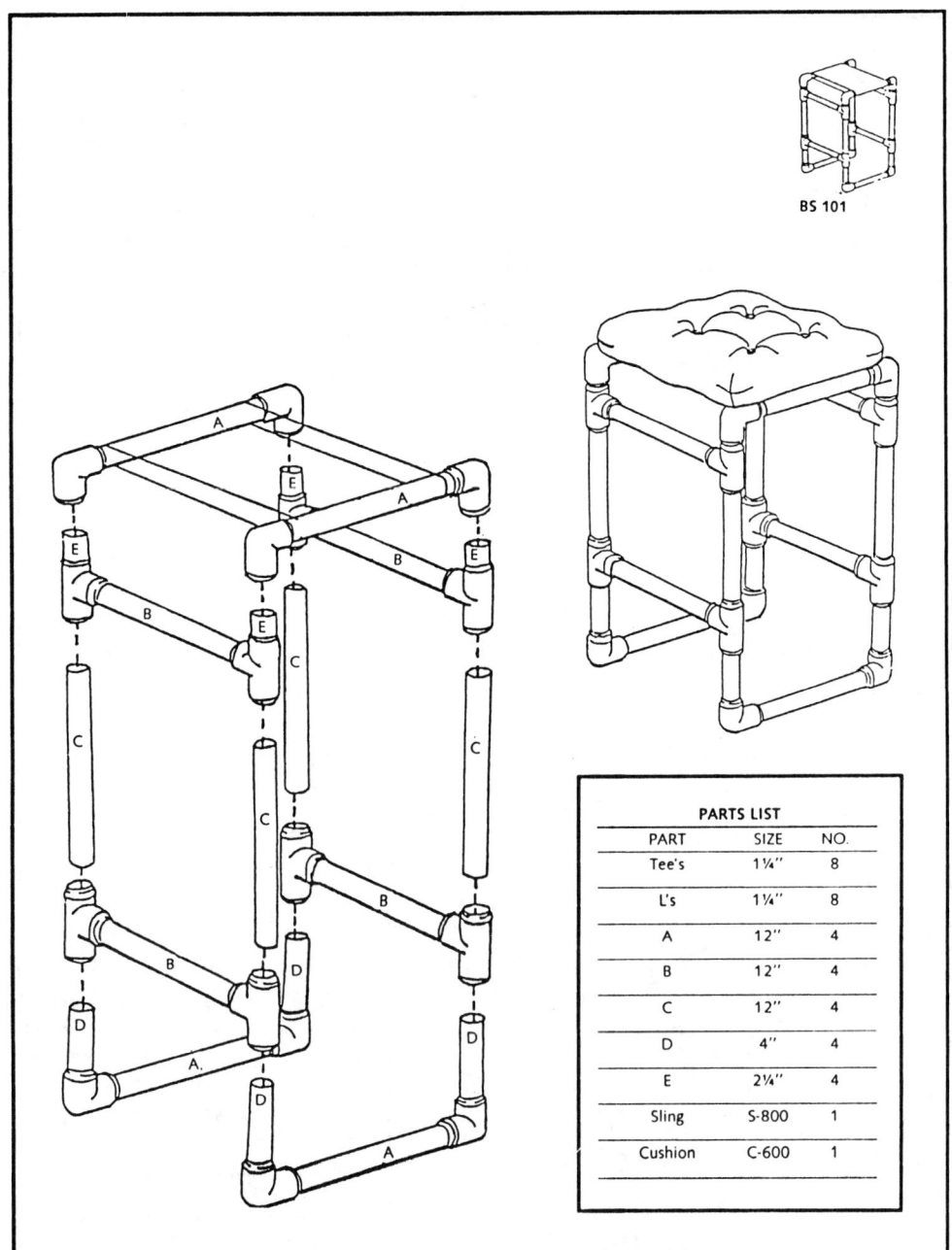

PARTS LIST

PART	SIZE	NO.
Tee's	1¼"	8
L's	1¼"	8
A	12"	4
B	12"	4
C	12"	4
D	4"	4
E	2¼"	4
Sling	S-800	1
Cushion	C-600	1

BAR STOOL
BS 102

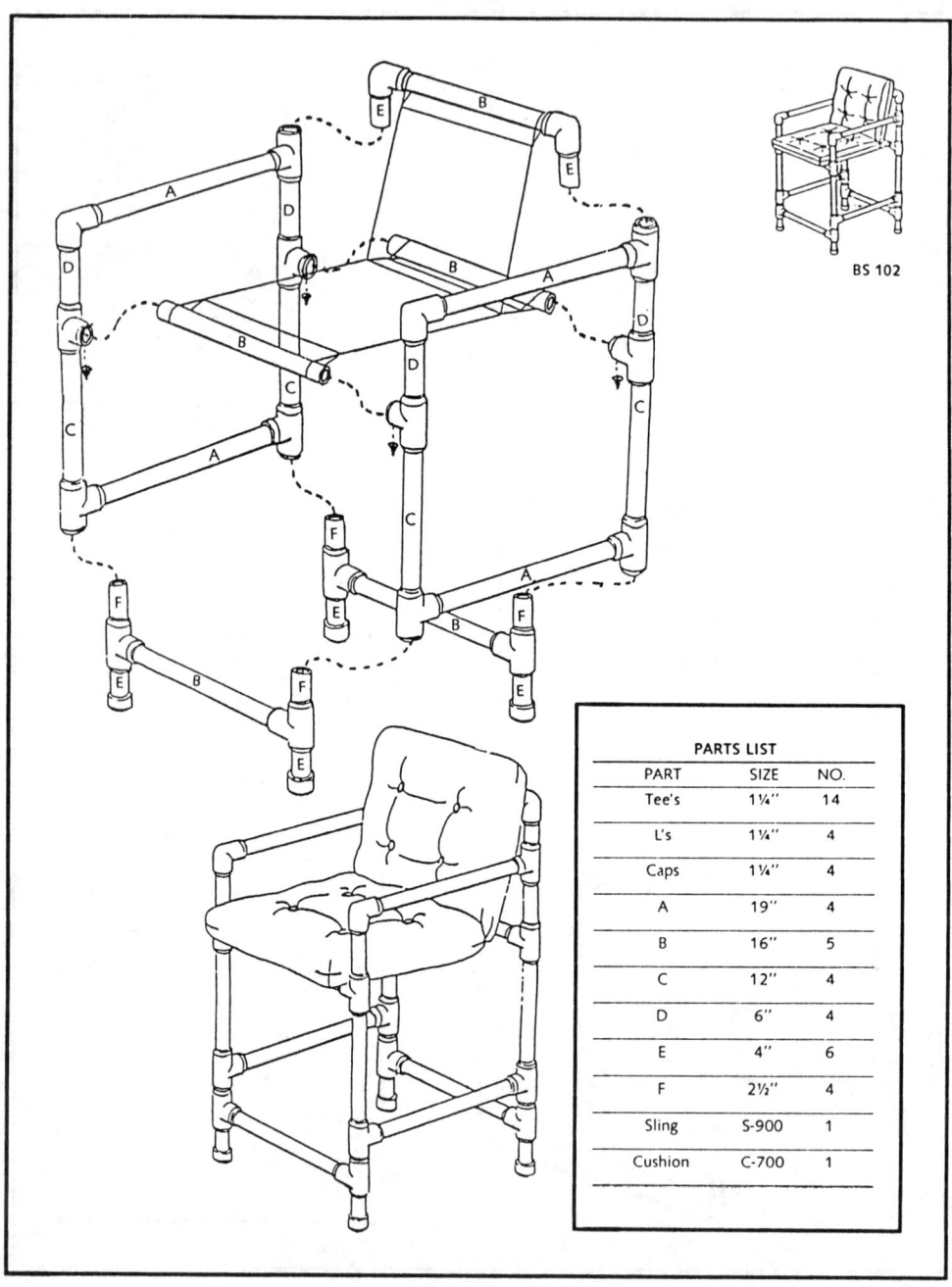

BS 102

PARTS LIST

PART	SIZE	NO.
Tee's	1¼"	14
L's	1¼"	4
Caps	1¼"	4
A	19"	4
B	16"	5
C	12"	4
D	6"	4
E	4"	6
F	2½"	4
Sling	S-900	1
Cushion	C-700	1

3
Indoor Chairs

DINING CHAIR
DC 101

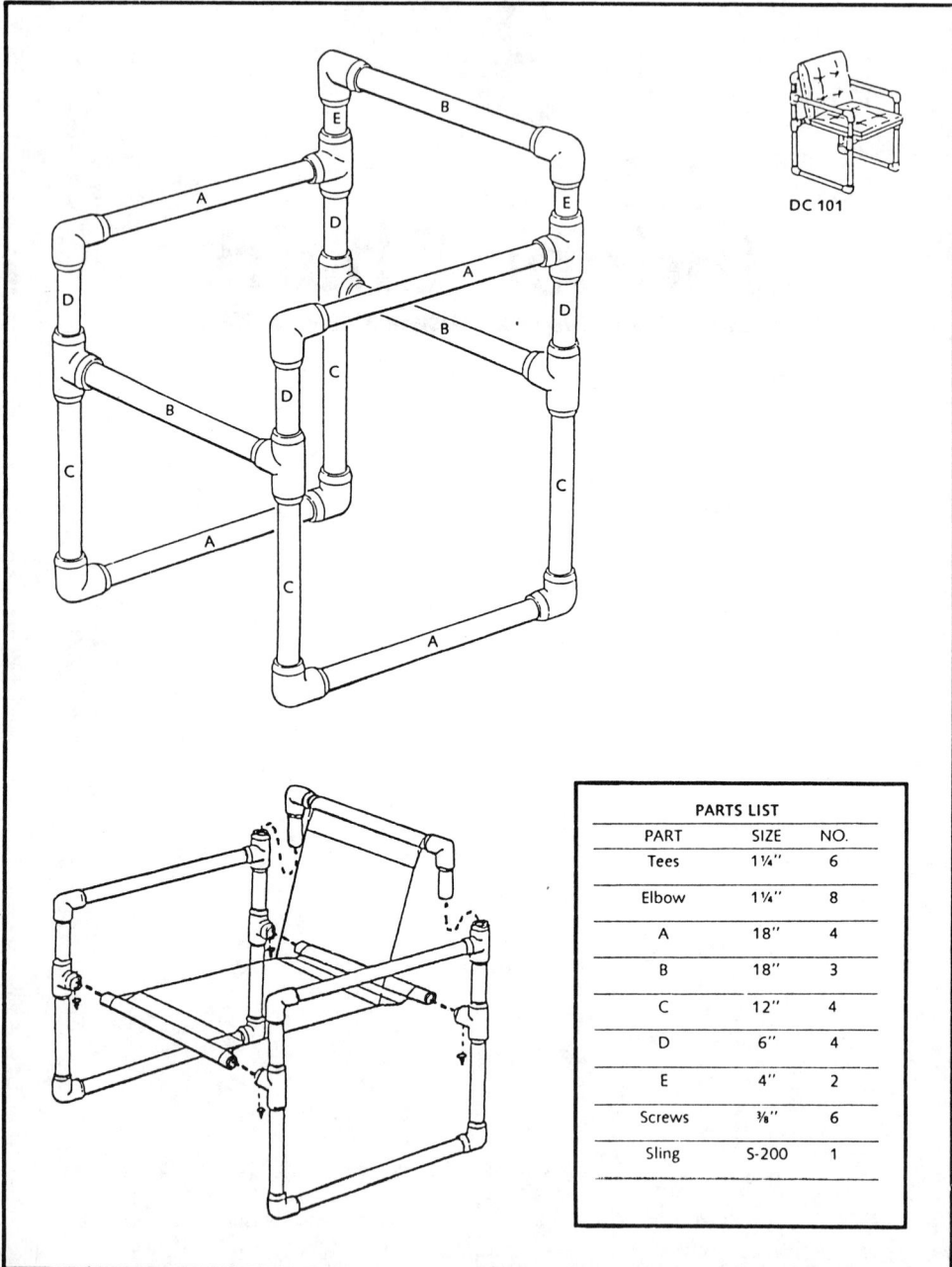

PARTS LIST		
PART	SIZE	NO.
Tees	1¼"	6
Elbow	1¼"	8
A	18"	4
B	18"	3
C	12"	4
D	6"	4
E	4"	2
Screws	⅜"	6
Sling	S-200	1

CLUB CHAIR
CC 101

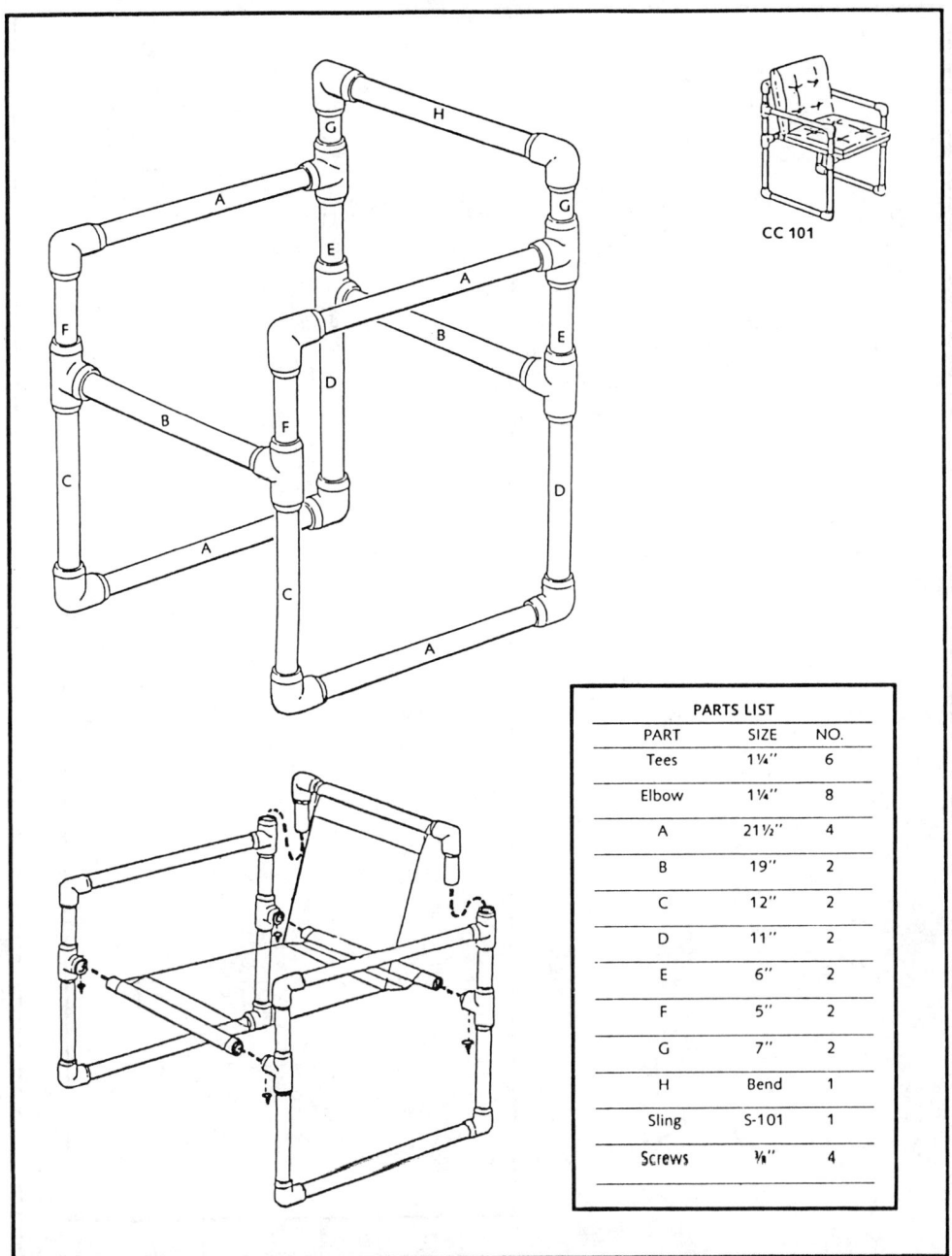

CC 101

PARTS LIST		
PART	SIZE	NO.
Tees	1¼"	6
Elbow	1¼"	8
A	21½"	4
B	19"	2
C	12"	2
D	11"	2
E	6"	2
F	5"	2
G	7"	2
H	Bend	1
Sling	S-101	1
Screws	⅜"	4

LOVE SEAT
LS 101 / LS 201

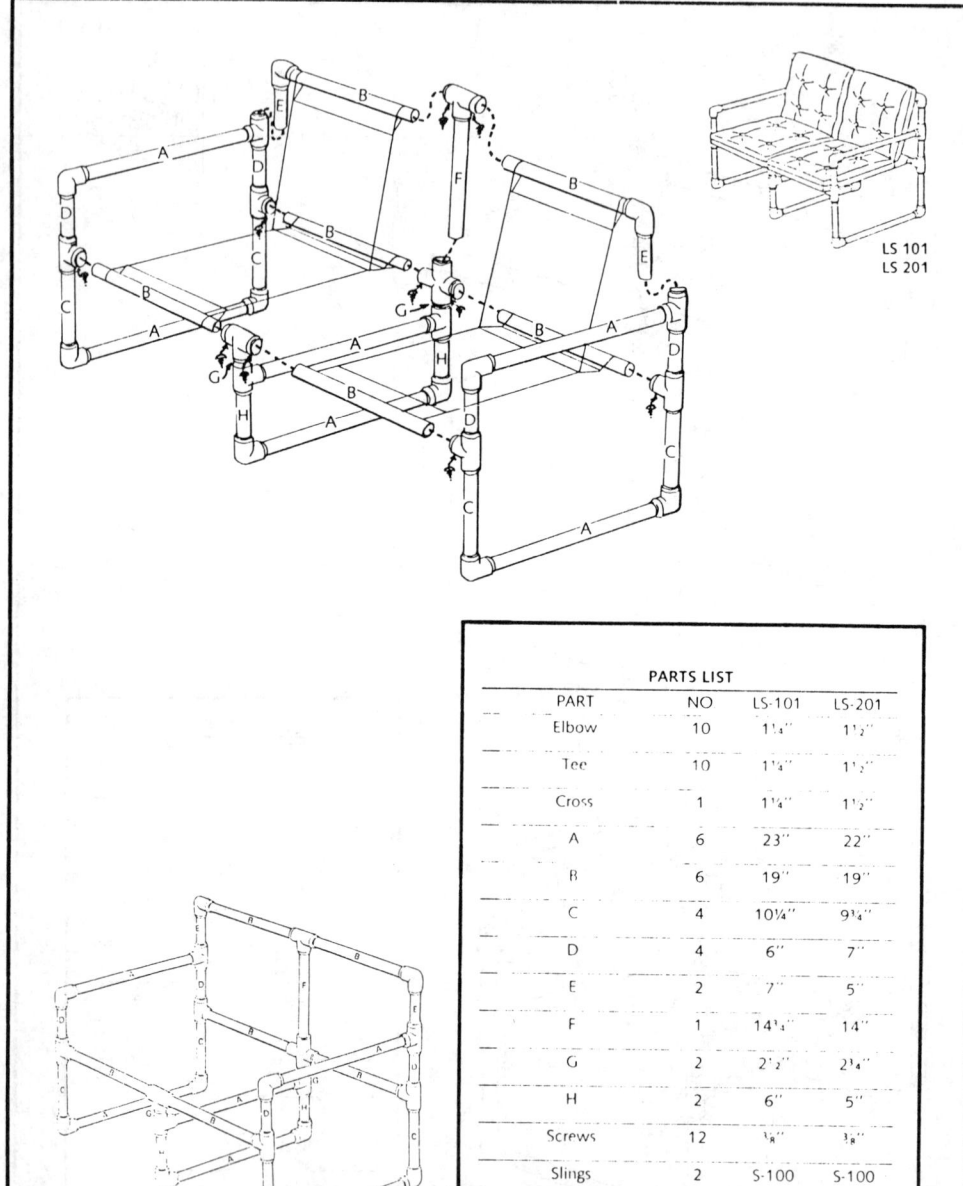

PARTS LIST			
PART	NO	LS-101	LS-201
Elbow	10	1¼"	1½"
Tee	10	1¼"	1½"
Cross	1	1¼"	1½"
A	6	23"	22"
B	6	19"	19"
C	4	10¼"	9¼"
D	4	6"	7"
E	2	7"	5"
F	1	14½"	14"
G	2	2½"	2¼"
H	2	6"	5"
Screws	12	⅜"	⅜"
Slings	2	S-100	S-100

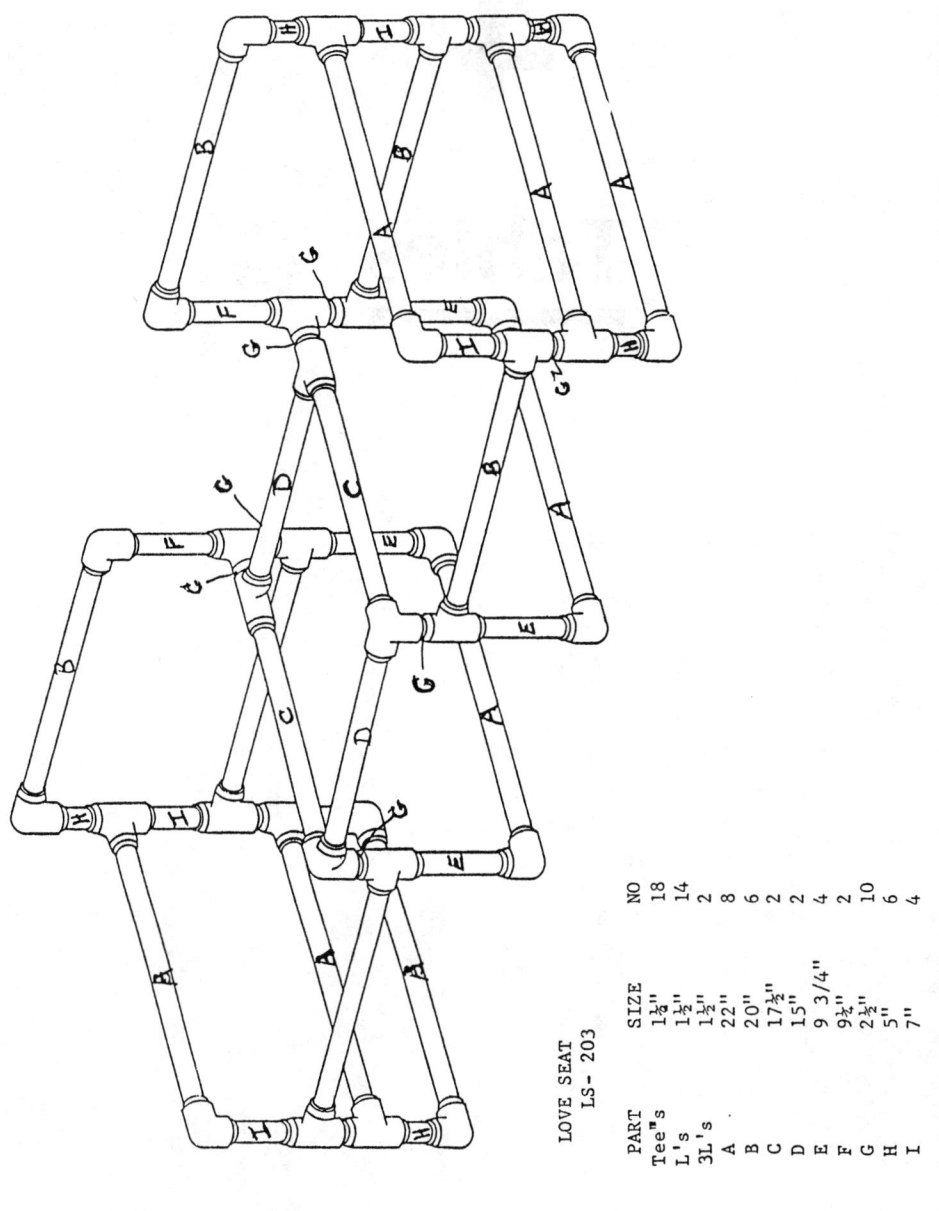

LOVE SEAT
LS- 203

PART	SIZE	NO
Tee"s	1½"	18
L's	1½"	14
3L's	1½"	2
A	22"	8
B	20"	6
C	17½"	2
D	15"	2
E	9 3/4"	4
F	9¾"	2
G	2¾"	10
H	5"	6
I	7"	4

4

Tables

COFFEE TABLE
CT 101/CT 201

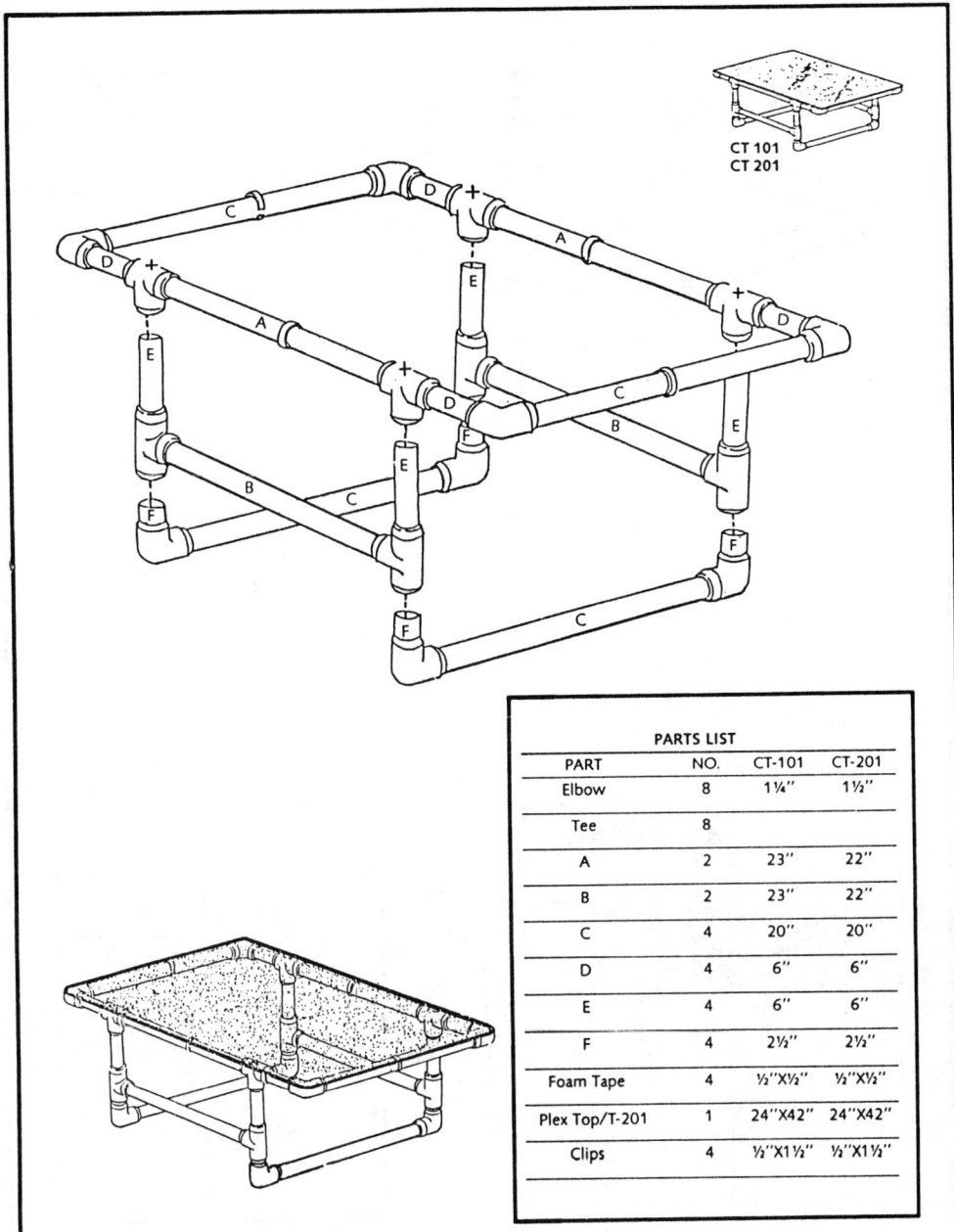

CT 101
CT 201

PARTS LIST			
PART	NO.	CT-101	CT-201
Elbow	8	1¼"	1½"
Tee	8		
A	2	23"	22"
B	2	23"	22"
C	4	20"	20"
D	4	6"	6"
E	4	6"	6"
F	4	2½"	2½"
Foam Tape	4	½"X½"	½"X½"
Plex Top/T-201	1	24"X42"	24"X42"
Clips	4	½"X1½"	½"X1½"

END TABLE
ET 102

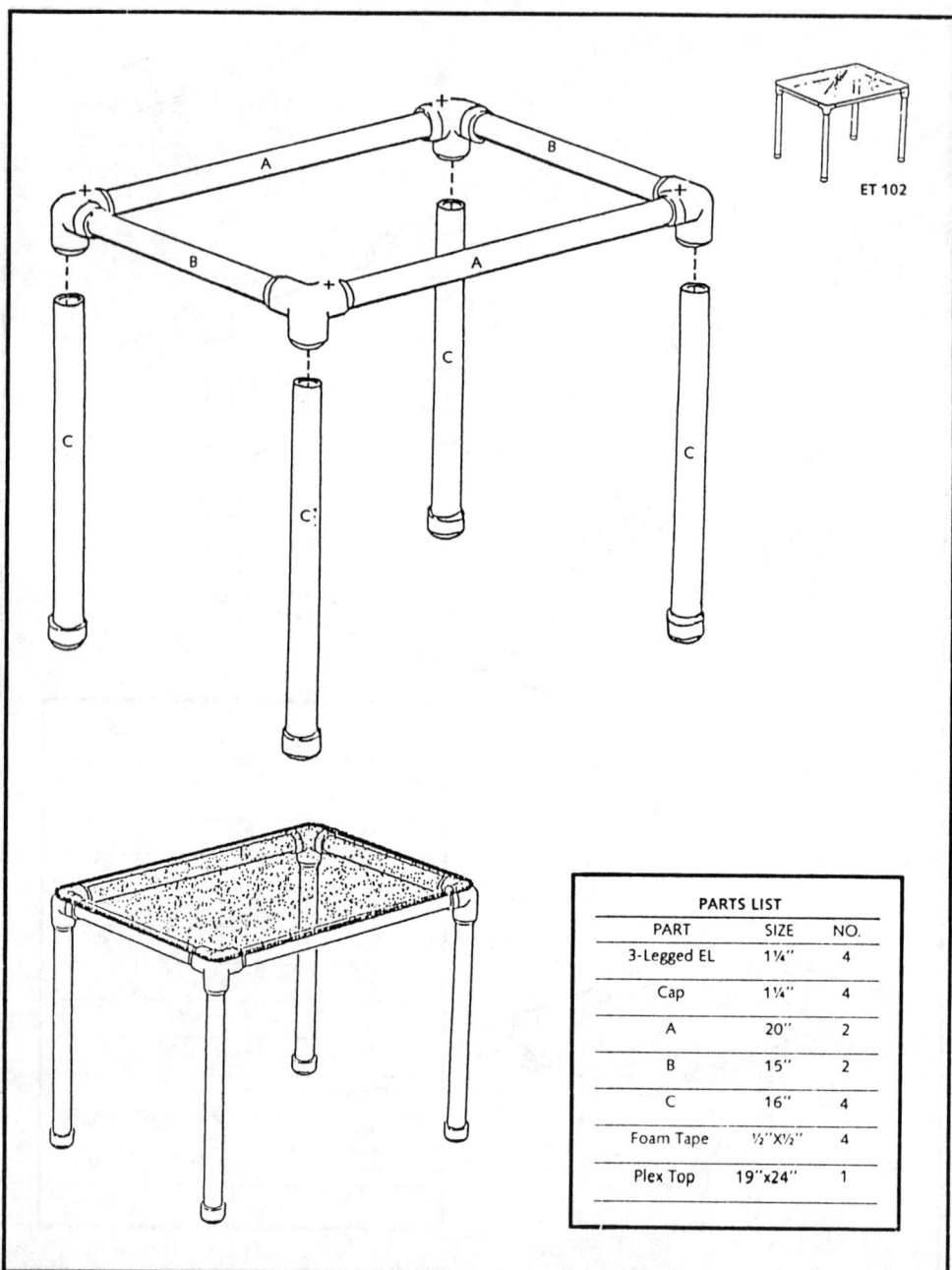

PARTS LIST		
PART	SIZE	NO.
3-Legged EL	1¼"	4
Cap	1¼"	4
A	20"	2
B	15"	2
C	16"	4
Foam Tape	½"X½"	4
Plex Top	19"x24"	1

END TABLE
ET 101/ET 201

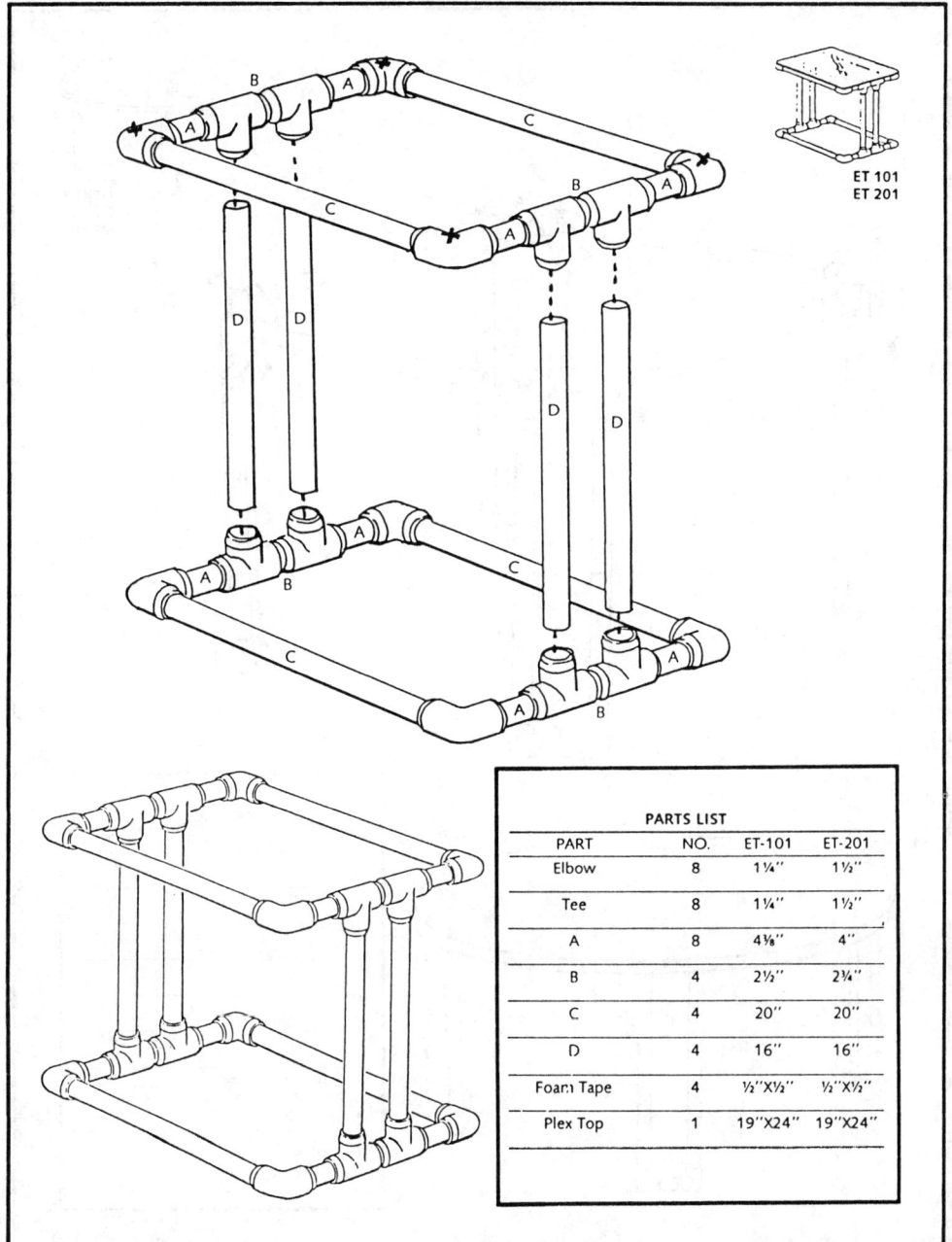

PARTS LIST			
PART	NO.	ET-101	ET-201
Elbow	8	1¼"	1½"
Tee	8	1¼"	1½"
A	8	4⅛"	4"
B	4	2½"	2¾"
C	4	20"	20"
D	4	16"	16"
Foam Tape	4	½"X½"	½"X½"
Plex Top	1	19"X24"	19"X24"

DINING TABLE
DT 103 / DT 104 / DT 105

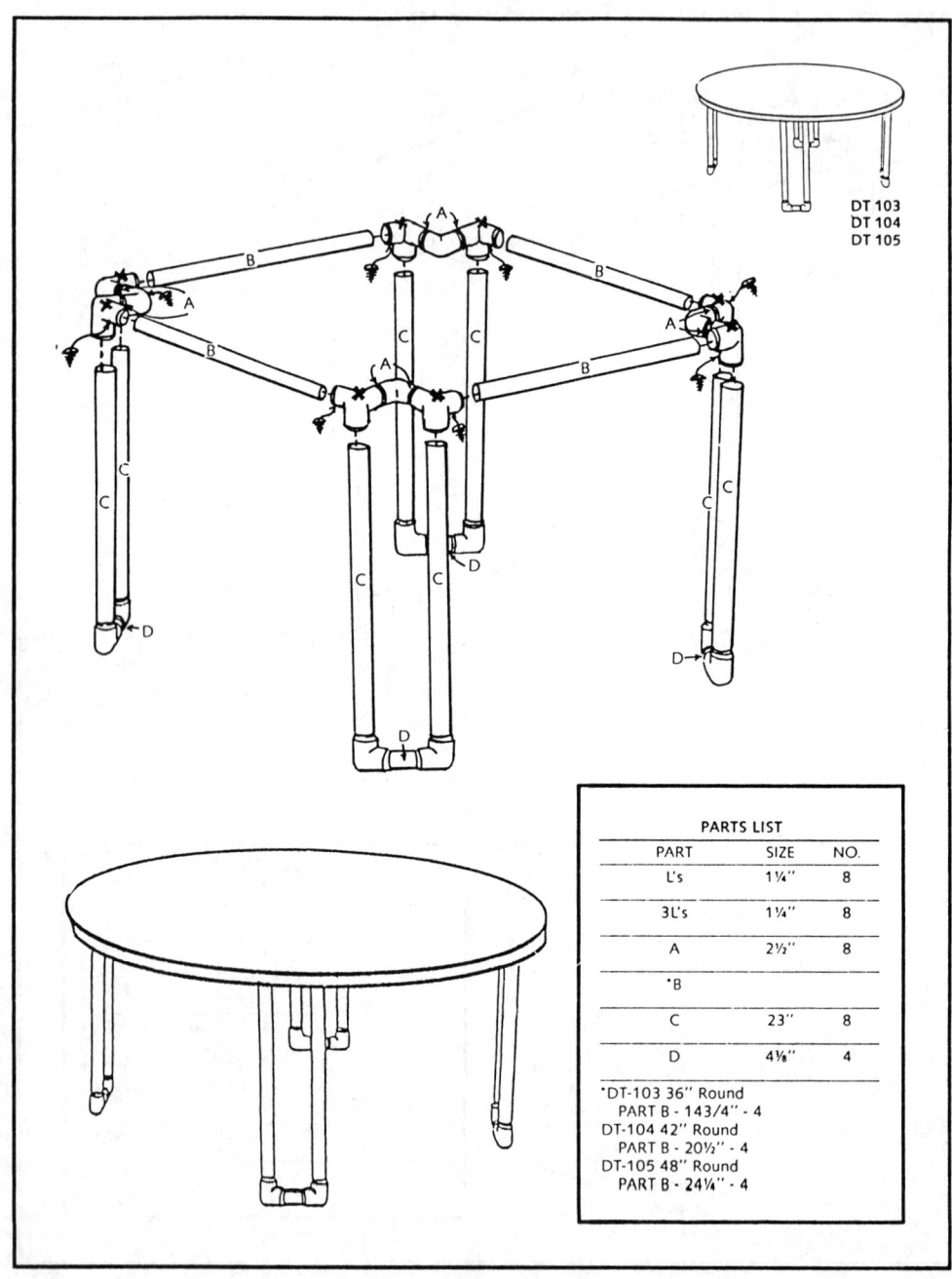

PARTS LIST		
PART	SIZE	NO.
L's	1¼"	8
3L's	1¼"	8
A	2½"	8
*B		
C	23"	8
D	4⅛"	4

*DT-103 36" Round
  PART B - 14¾" - 4
DT-104 42" Round
  PART B - 20½" - 4
DT-105 48" Round
  PART B - 24¼" - 4

DINING TABLE
DT 102

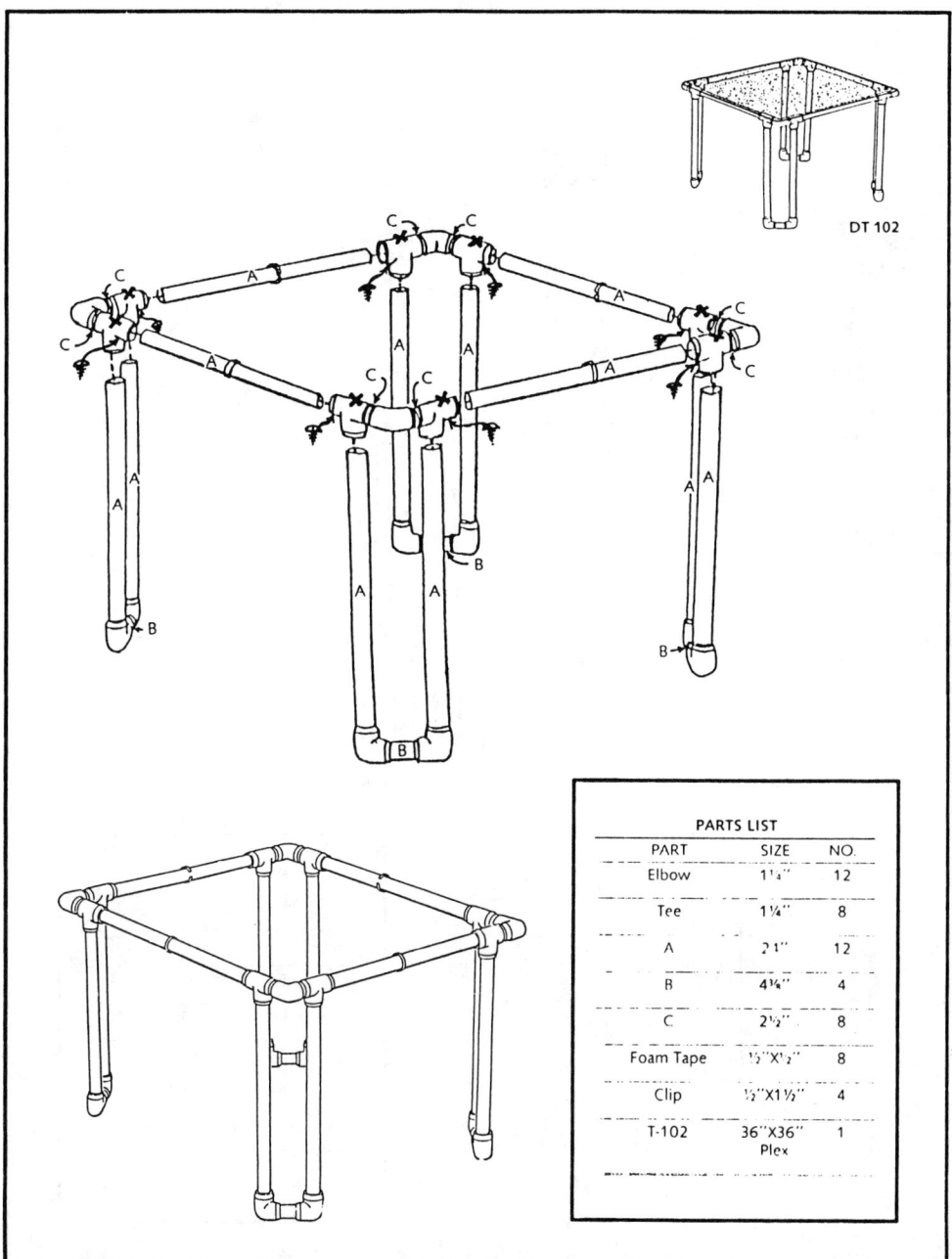

PARTS LIST		
PART	SIZE	NO.
Elbow	1¼"	12
Tee	1¼"	8
A	21"	12
B	4¼"	4
C	2½"	8
Foam Tape	½"X½"	8
Clip	½"X1½"	4
T-102	36"X36" Plex	1

DINING TABLE
DT 101

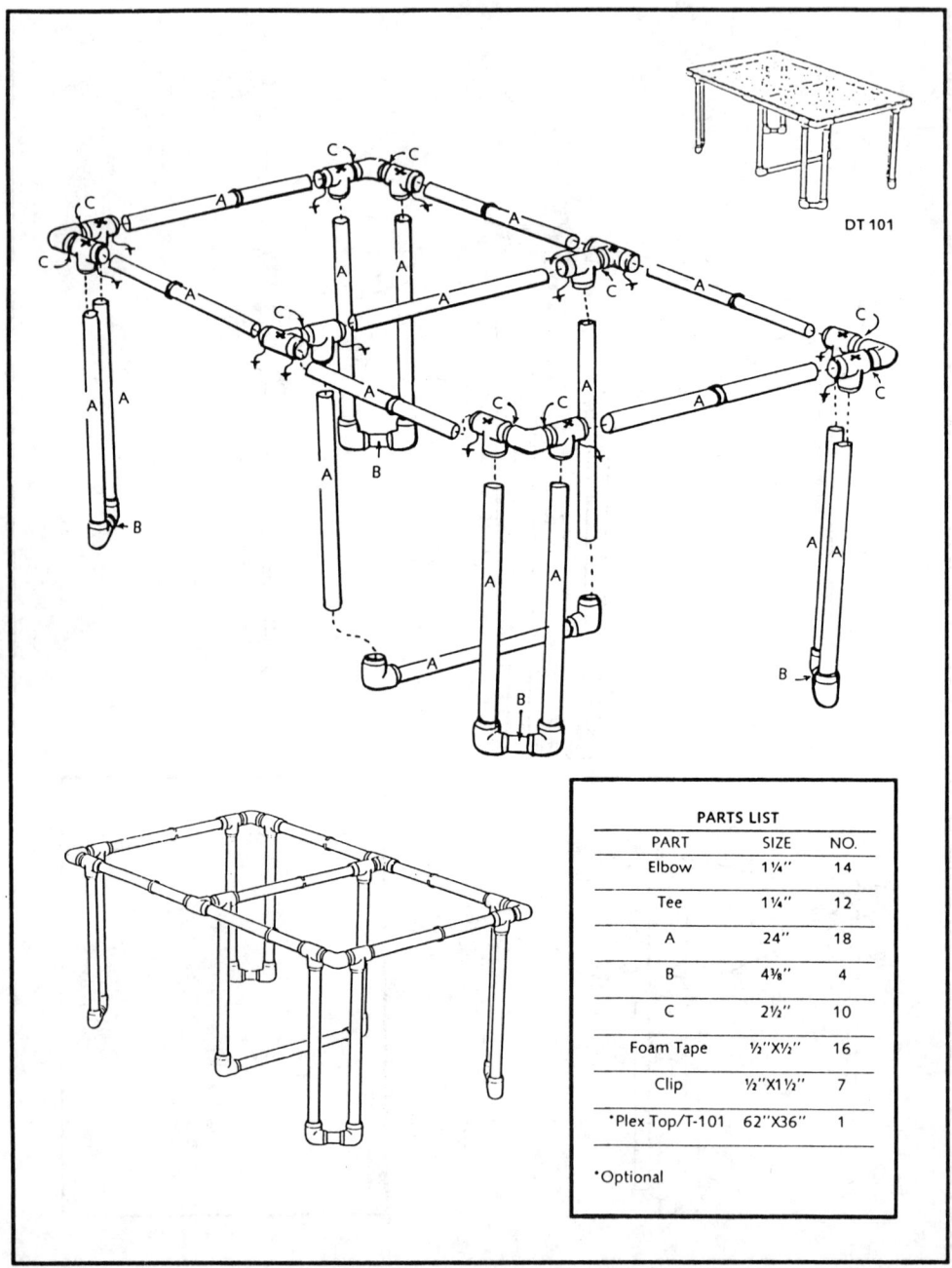

PARTS LIST		
PART	SIZE	NO.
Elbow	1¼"	14
Tee	1¼"	12
A	24"	18
B	4⅛"	4
C	2½"	10
Foam Tape	½"X½"	16
Clip	½"X1½"	7
*Plex Top/T-101	62"X36"	1

*Optional

5

Glider Chairs

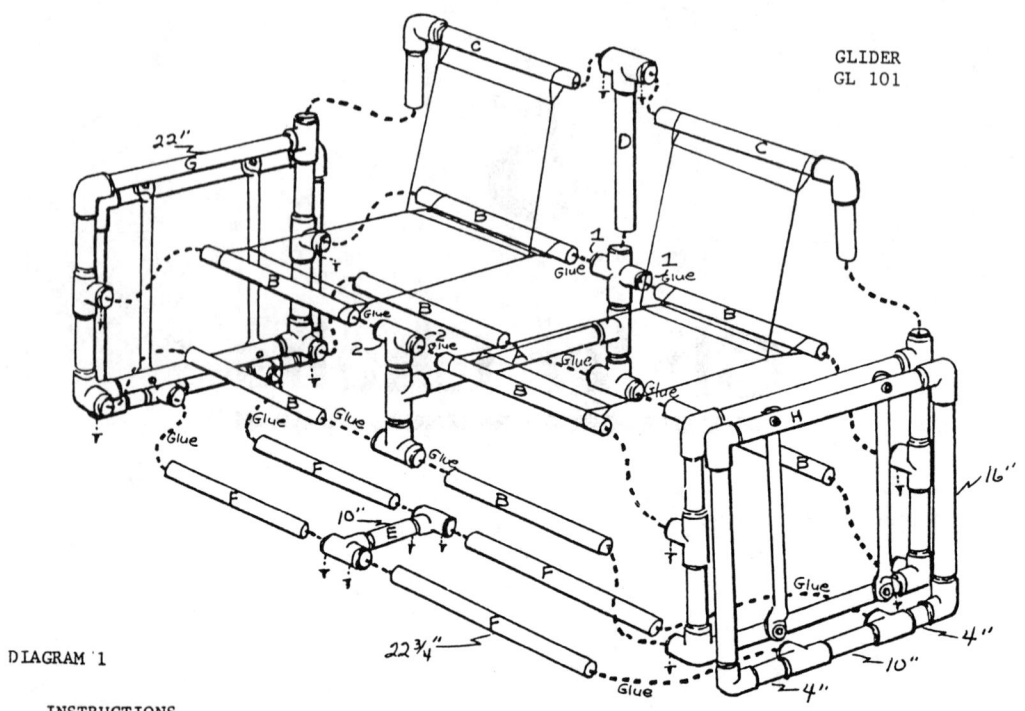

DIAGRAM 1

GLIDER
GL 101

INSTRUCTIONS

It is preferrable to assemble on a flat padded surface.
Refer often to the diagrams.
It will be necessary to glue certain parts. Follow the instructions carefully as all bonds are permanent.
Work in a well-ventilated area while gluing.
All pipes should sit firmly in their sockets.

1. Take PART "A". Note that one end has an extra open socket. Rest PART "A" on a flat surface with the extra open socket away from you and pointing straight up.
2. Carefully unroll a SLING so that the pipes do not slip out. Grasp the pipe with an elbow (PIPE "C") and hold the SLING in front of you so that the SLING hangs straight down. The middle pipe should be through a loop in the shortest flap and should be hanging in the back.
3. Look at the PIPE "C" in the SLING. Is the elbow on the right or left? If it is on the right, the SLING will be fitted to the right side of PART "A". If on the left, the SLING will be fitted to the left side of PART "A". Place the sling on the correct side.
4. There are two "B" PIPES inserted in two of the SLING loops. The end of PIPE "B" that is in the short flap loop connects to SOCKET 1. The end of the other PIPE "B" connects to SOCKET 2. Remember, the "C" PART must be positioned so that the elbow is away from PART "A".
5. It is necessary to glue the "B" PIPES into SOCKETS 1 and 2. It may be easier to lay PART "A" on the open sockets opposite the ones being glued. When bonded, return to the original position. Follow Steps 6 and 7 carefully, they explain the gluing process.
6. The glue you are about to use forms a permanent bond between PVC pieces. It is necessary to work quickly once the glue is applied to a surface. Read the instructions on the glue container. Have a box of tissues or other dispoable type wiping cloths within easy reach. To form the best bond, glue will be applied to both surfaces. Read the procedure in Step 7 before gluing.

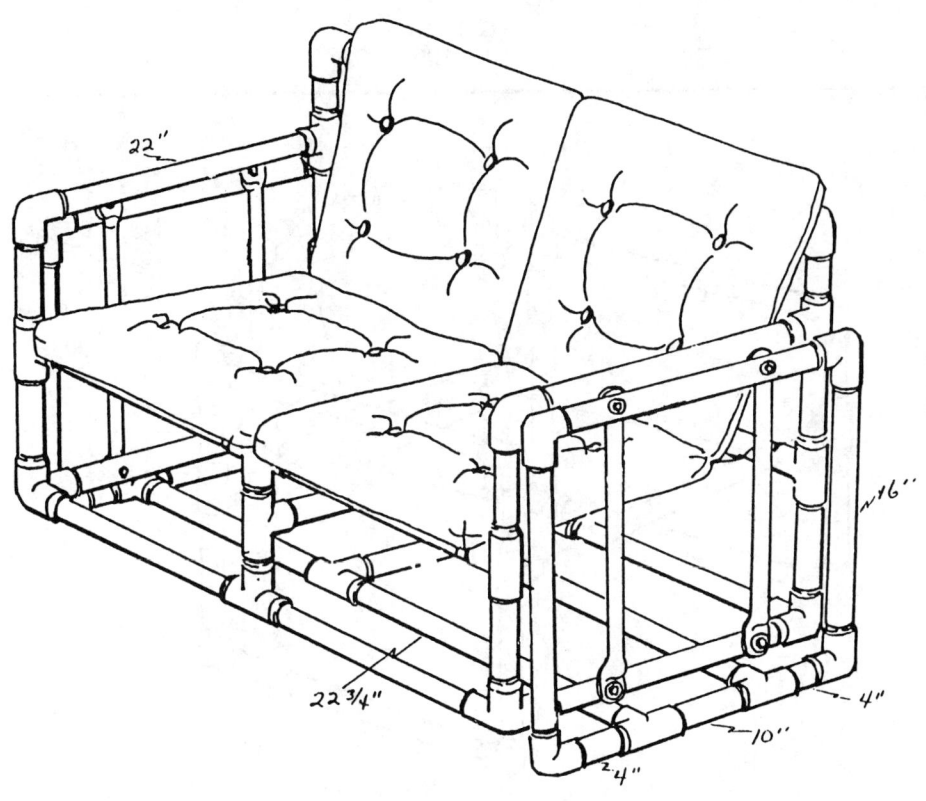

DIAGRAM 2

INVENTORY	
PART	QUANTITY
A	1
B	8
C	2
D	1
E	1
F	4
G	1
H	1
Slings	2
Cushions	2
Screws	14
Glue	1

SEE PAGE 16F
SWING SEAT SW101
FOR DIMENSIONS

GLIDER
GL 102

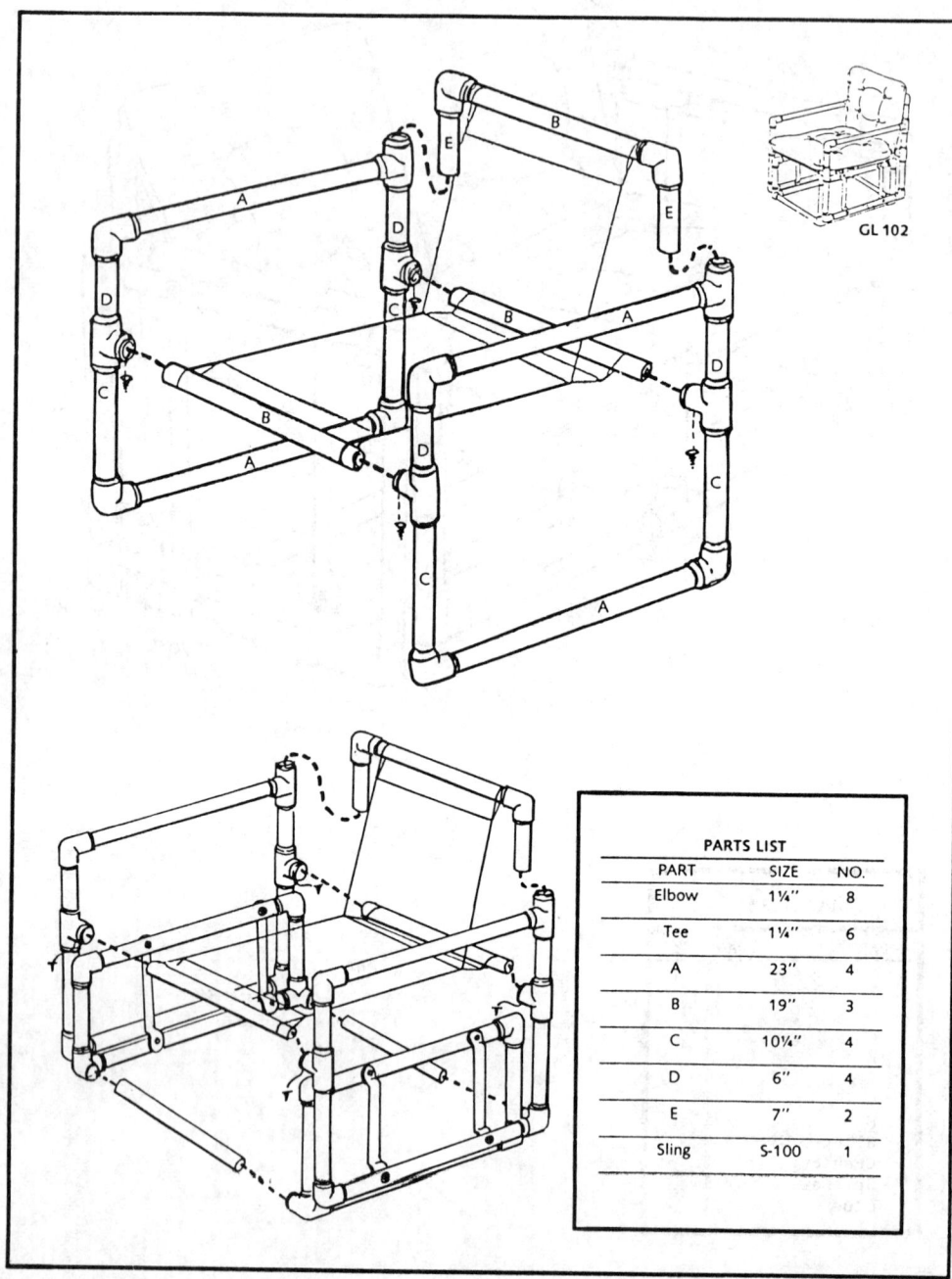

BASE
GL 102

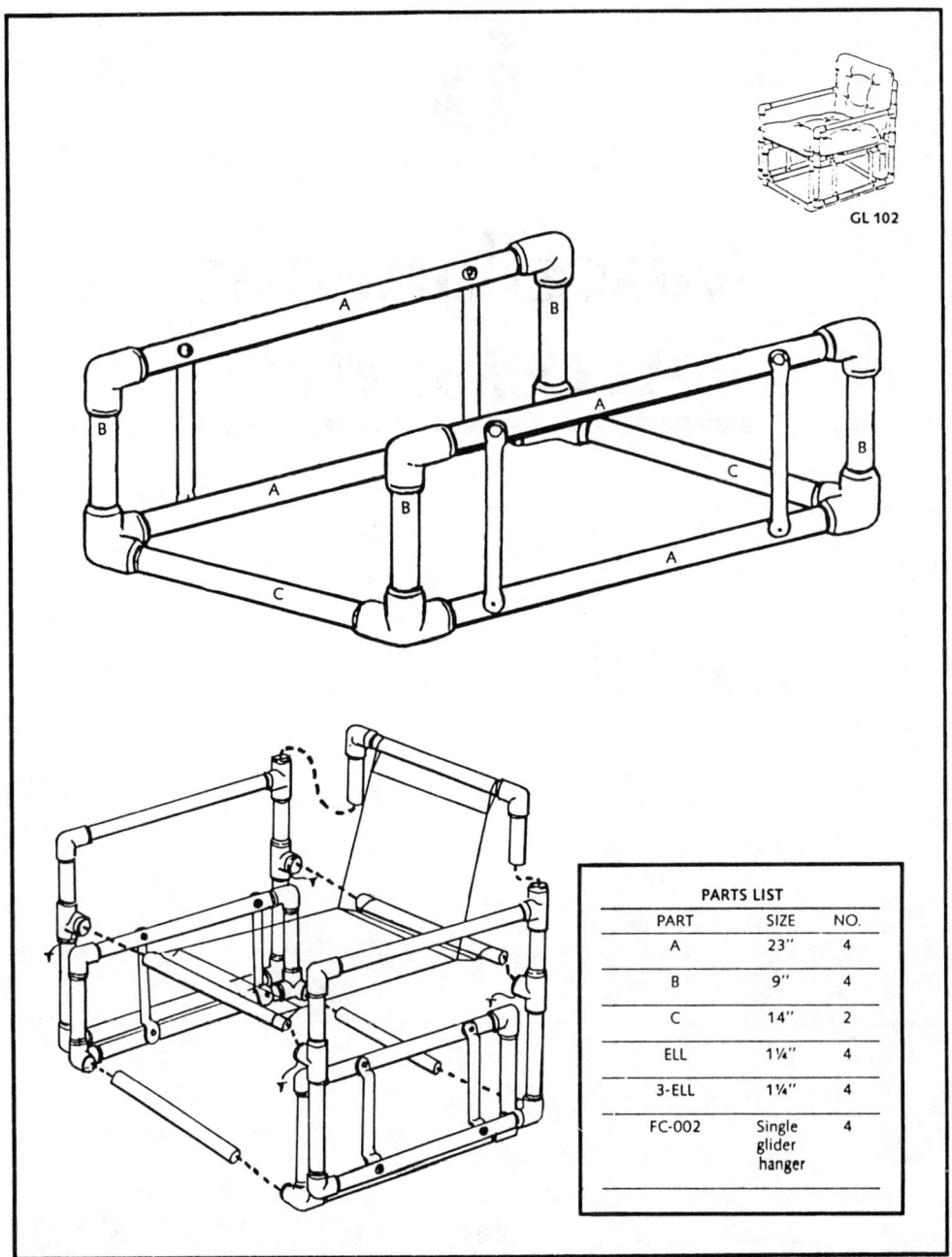

PARTS LIST		
PART	SIZE	NO.
A	23"	4
B	9"	4
C	14"	2
ELL	1¼"	4
3-ELL	1¼"	4
FC-002	Single glider hanger	4

6

Miscellaneous Accessories

OTTMAN
OT-101

PARTS LIST

Part	Size	No.
Elbow	1¼"	4
Tee	1¼"	10
A	15¼"	3
B	6¾"	8
C	8"	4
D	2½"	8
Glue	¼ pt	1
Sling	OT	1

OT101

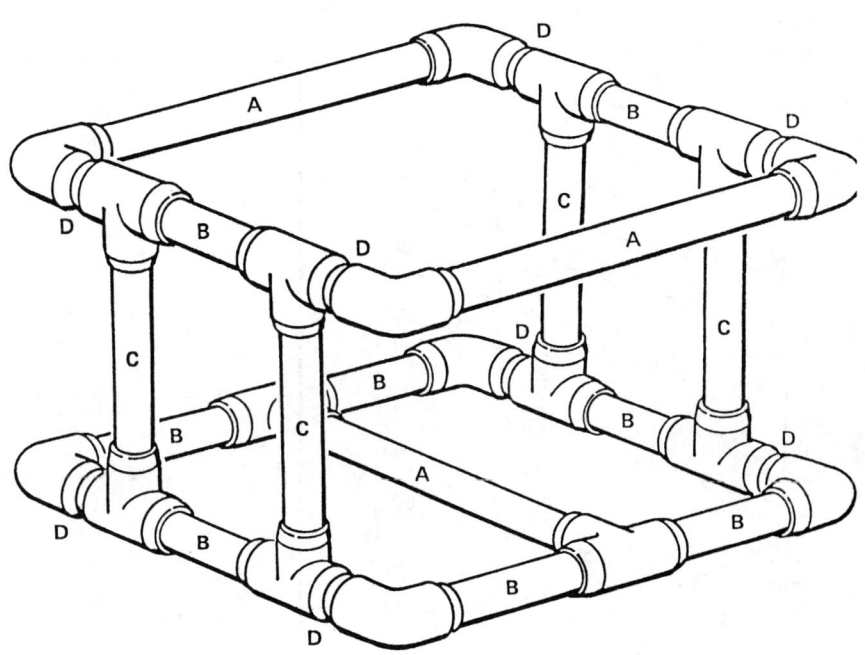

MOBILE SERVER
MS 101

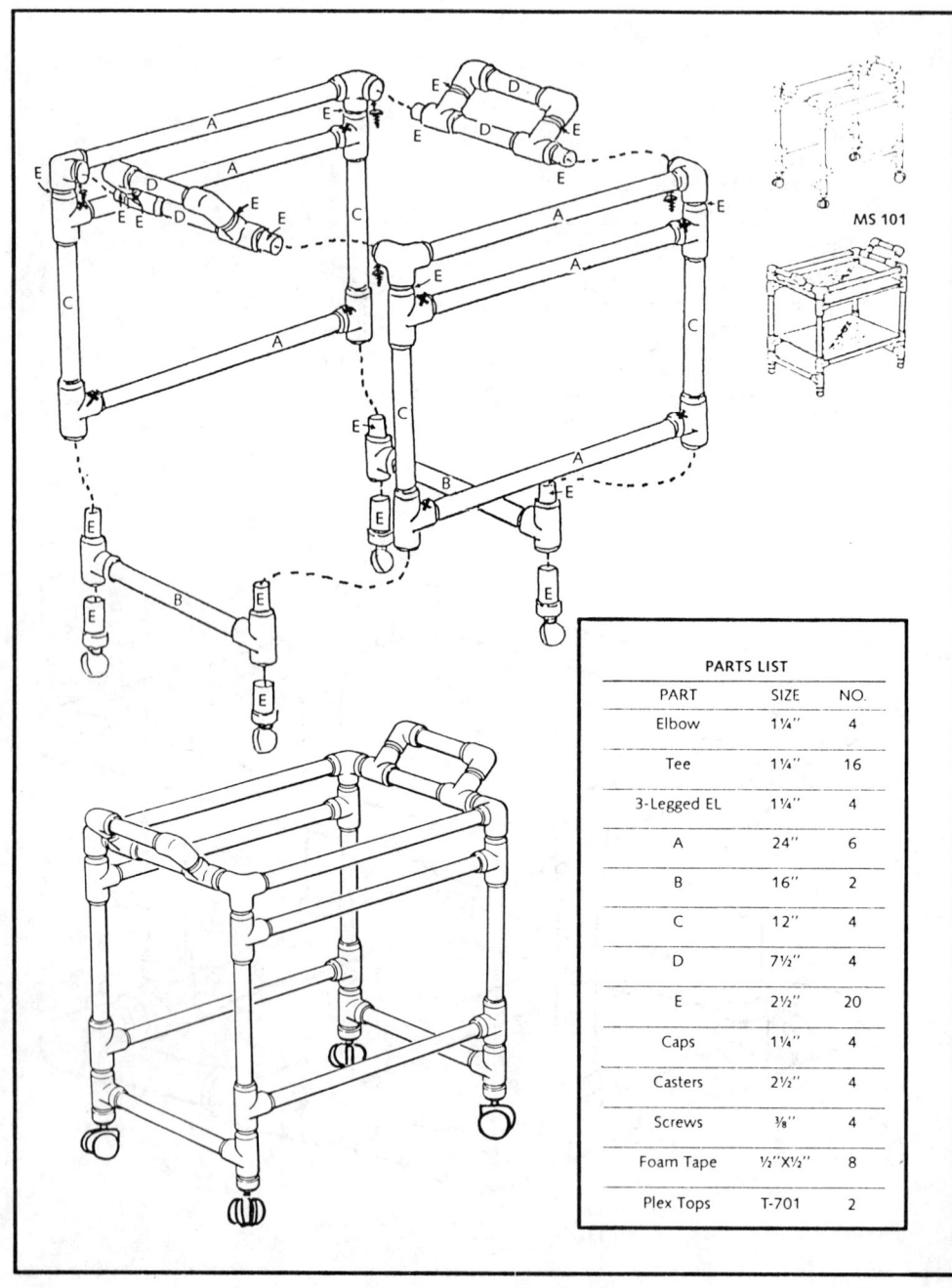

PARTS LIST		
PART	SIZE	NO.
Elbow	1¼"	4
Tee	1¼"	16
3-Legged EL	1¼"	4
A	24"	6
B	16"	2
C	12"	4
D	7½"	4
E	2½"	20
Caps	1¼"	4
Casters	2½"	4
Screws	⅜"	4
Foam Tape	½"X½"	8
Plex Tops	T-701	2

PLANT STAND
PS 101

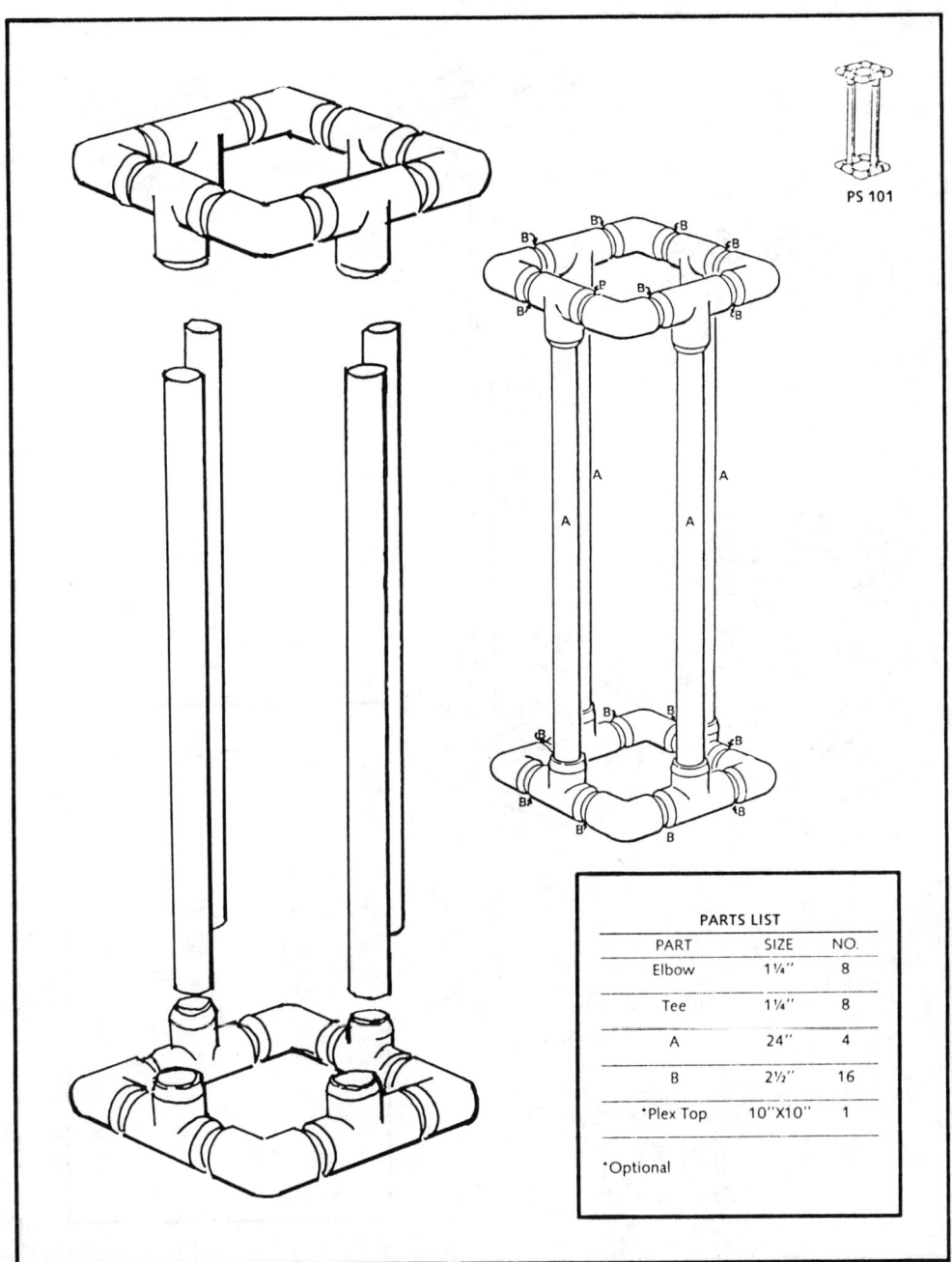

PARTS LIST		
PART	SIZE	NO.
Elbow	1¼"	8
Tee	1¼"	8
A	24"	4
B	2½"	16
*Plex Top	10"X10"	1

*Optional

PLANT STAND
PS 102

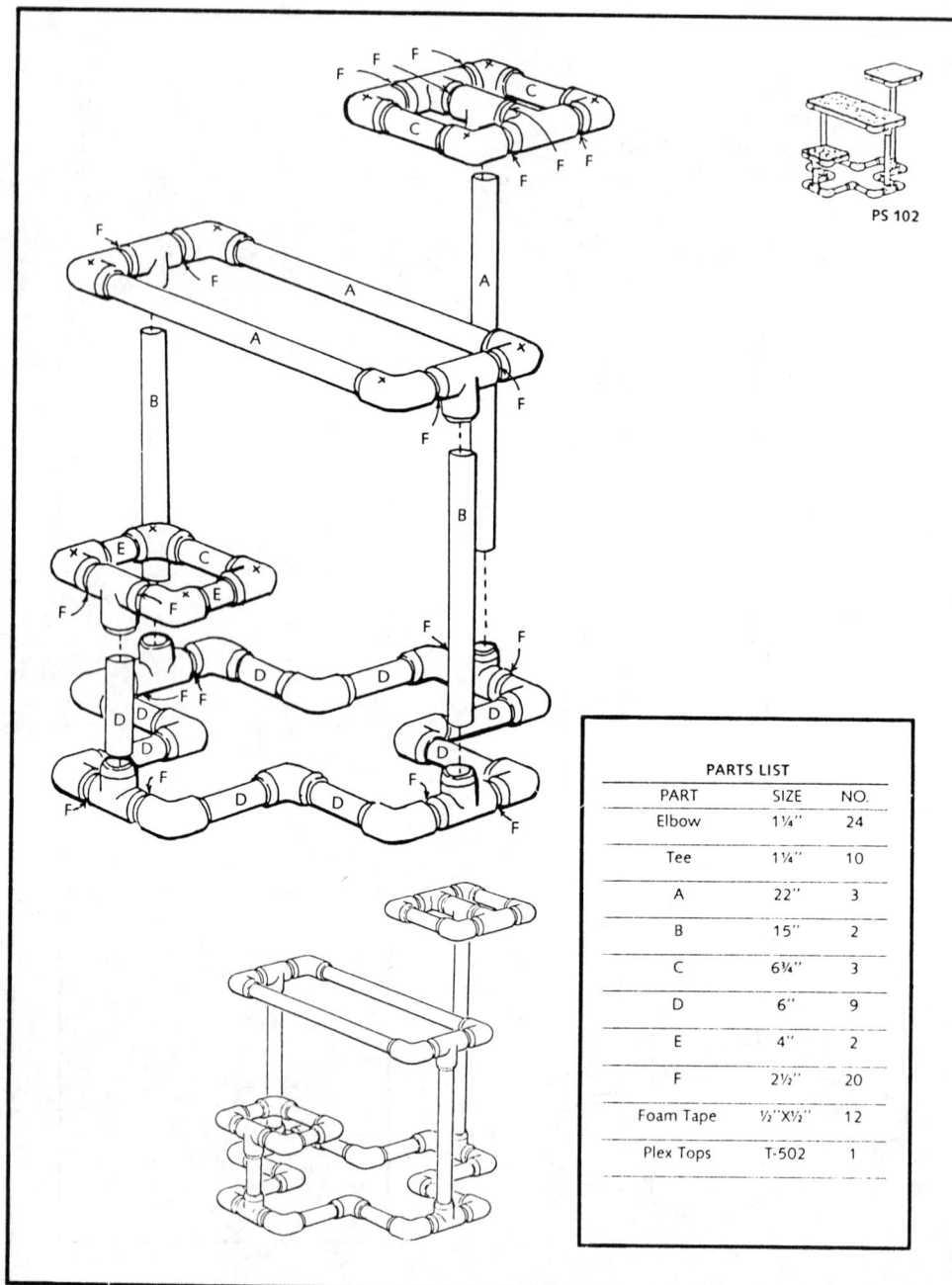

PARTS LIST		
PART	SIZE	NO.
Elbow	1¼"	24
Tee	1¼"	10
A	22"	3
B	15"	2
C	6¼"	3
D	6"	9
E	4"	2
F	2½"	20
Foam Tape	½"X½"	12
Plex Tops	T-502	1

Making Money With Stained Glass

Stained glass offers you the chance to make money with something easy and beautiful to make. Everyone loves stained glass. But not everyone knows how to make stained glass. This section of this book will show you how you can make beautiful stained glass art pieces at a low cost. And, you can probably sell the same piece for as much as ten times what you paid to produce it. You will be surprised at what beauty your hands can and will create with this guide.

Stained glass is an art form that has been around for centuries. It was first used in churches as far back as 969 A.D. Recently, though, the art has become popular as a secular form of art. Now stained glass is seen in banks, hotels, restaurants, as well as in the home.

To learn various techniques, you may want to check with local colleges and schools to see if they offer courses in stained glass.

Here is a step-by-step process that describes the tools and materials needed, where they are available, and how to create your own stained glass.

It's a good idea to read this book before you buy the required tools. Also, as a beginner, you won't need to have all the necessary equipment — some alternatives are provided.

The tools and equipment needed for stained glass projects are found in crafts stores and are usually not that expensive.

Tools Needed

One of the most important tools you'll need is a glass cutter. The most commonly used ones are Diamantor, Red Devil #023 and a Fletcher #02. The handles and shapes of the cutters will vary in size and shape, so make sure you choose cutters that are designed for the type of glass you're using. Also, make sure they're comfortable in your hand.

Other necessary tools you'll need to purchase are the soldering iron and tips which are available in hardware stores. A 3/8" diameter tip is probably the best choice to begin with. It's best to use an 80-200 watt iron. If the iron does not include a stand, it's important to buy one. The purpose of the stand is to keep the iron off the table.

A came (or lead) knife is for cutting lead came. Lead came is what will hold the stained glass pieces together. Came knives are available in hardware stores. You'll also need to buy X-acto and matte knives.

A stright-edge ruler (preferably a metal one) and a 45-degree triangle are needed for cutting and measuring.

You'll need a small can of household oil to lubricate the glass cutter wheels and to sharpen the caming knife.

Flat wide-nosed pliers are needed to clip off small glass pieces and chips on the edge of the glass.

Horseshoe nails and a medium-sized hammer are for holding the glass in place while you're leading. Instead of horseshoe nails, you may use what are known as 16- to 18-gauge brads.

Lathekins are flat wooden tools used to smooth the lead joints in leaded stained glass projects or to polish and smooth copper foil. These are found in craft or stained glass supply stores. Otherwise, you can just use a 3/8" dowel with a blunt point.

A carborundum stone and a steel file are used to smooth the edges on the glass and sharpen the came knife. These are available in hardware stores.

A moist cellulose sponge is good for cleaning off the tip of the soldering iron.

For the copper foil technique, you'll need copper foil wrapping. This foil is available in adhesive-backed rolls which are three feet long. You may choose among widths of 3/16, 1/4, 3/8, and 1/2 of an inch wide, depending on the thickness of the glass pieces in your project.

For leaded stained glass projects, you'll need to buy strips of lead came. Came is a grooved strip of pliable lead that holds individual sections of glass in its channels.

Soldering paste and oleic acid flux are needed for the lead and copper foil stained glass techniques. Flux is a material, often liquid, that gets rid of oxides from the metal. The flux helps solder flow and form a strong joint between the pieces.

Solder is sold in the form of wire on spools or by the bar. Wire is easier to work with, and the most common size is the 1/8-inch and 1/16-inch solid wire. Solder is usually mixed in a proportion of 60 percent tin to 40 percent lead. Sometimes you'll find a 50-50 mix. Don't buy liquid solder; although it sounds as if you can use it, it's not used in stained glass work.

Now for the most important material: the glass. Glass is sold by the sheet in various sizes. Stock sheets are usually 32 by 84 inches, but you can also purchase these in half and quarter sheets. Usually sheets are sold by the square foot.

When choosing glass for your project, select all the colors at the same time. Look for warps, bubbles, nicks, or other imperfections. If you've never worked with glass before, it's best to use antique glass — it's easier to cut than most other types of glass. Avoid yellows, reds, and oranges — these colors are brittle and difficult for beginners to cut.

Stained glass varies in thickness, texture, color, and hardness. If the glass you've selected has some imperfections, don't let the flaws throw you.

Test glass by tapping it with your fingers. If there's a dull 'thud,' you don't want this glass — it may crack easily.

There are two kinds of glass that are the most common in stained glass projects: handblown, or 'antique' glass, and machine-made, or 'rolled' glass. Hand-blown has a softer texture, making it easier to cut than machine-made glass; however, it is more costly. Hand-blown and machine-made glass is colored when the glass is being manufactured. This is done by adding chemicals and metals such as copper, chromium, even gold to the glass to tint it. The glass is never actually 'stained.'

Choose your glass for its texture as well as for the color.

These are the most important tools needed; other tools such as a dimmer switch for the soldering iron, a lead vise, finishing agents for the lead, and glazing putty are helpful but not required for beginning projects.

Cutting The Stained Glass

First find a work place. Make sure you put plenty of newspapers around and have a wisk broom handy — glass splinters can be dangerous. Also, make certain the working surface doesn't wobble.

It is recommended that you wear glasses, goggles, or some type of eye protection.

Now decide on a pattern. Start with a simple design that has mostly straight edges. Also it's a good idea to use just a few colors so you get the feel of the glass. Use inexpensive glass starting out.

This is the tricky part. The first attempts may be frustrating. You should first practice on a piece of scrap glass — a piece of window pane is good and it's less costly.

The cutter is the most important tool for cutting glass. Cutters with steel wheels work best. Keep your cutter in a small jar of a mixture of oil and turpentine soaked in cotton. Dip the cutter in this mixture every three or four cuts — this keeps it clean and keeps it from dulling. When the cutter becomes too dull, don't use it — buy a new one. They're not too expensive.

The cutter may feel a little awkward, since it tends to skip across the glass. But with some practice, it will get easier.

Holding your cutter is important for scoring. Scoring refers to the technique of scratching the glass so that it breaks perfectly. There are two methods — choose one that's comfortable. For the first method, hold the cutter between the your thumb and index fingers. Your two fingers should bear down on the shoulders of the cutter. Make sure the cutter is perpendicular to the glass. It's best to stand while cutting. Apply even pressure and cut along the entire length of the score.

For the second method, grasp the edge handle with all four fingers, placing the thumb on the top. The notched edge of the cutter should be perpendicular to the glass. Sometimes this second method gives you more control.

Now you're ready to score the glass. This means you will be scratching the surface of the glass with the glass cutter so that the glass will break along the line.

To score your glass, apply pressure on the cutter, starting at an 1/8 of an inch from the edge farthest from you. Listen to the 'hiss' of the cutter. Make sure you don't go off the edge of the glass, and NEVER go over the same score twice. The score should show clearly on the glass; if not, you need to apply more pressure. Always score the most difficult curves, lines, and shapes in your pattern first. After each score, break apart the glass.

Now you need to start a 'run' in the score which is done by tapping the score lines. A run is when the glass cracks in a line. The run should follow the score line. Hold the scored piece of glass in one hand and the cutter in the other. With the end of the cutter, gently tap the underside of the score. Start at the edge and tap toward the middle. This will start the run, and once the run starts, keep tapping just in front of it. Tap firmly, but not too forceful, and only do this over the work bench.

To break off straight scores, make a fist with both your hands. Clench your fingers under the glass, placing your thumbs on top, thumbs on top, parallel to the top of the score. Press firmly with one hand, and with the other hand, grasp the edge and snap down.

Another method is to use a ruler. Place the score just over the edge of the ruler. Put one hand on each side of the ruler and press the glass firmly down.

Pliers can help snap off small straight line scores, too. Place a piece of cloth between the pliers and the glass piece. Pull down and away from the glass with the pliers.

Grozing pliers work best for snapping off thin pieces of glass. Grozing pliers make the job faster, and there is less chance of your glass breaking. The purpose of using the pliers is to even out the edges so that when it comes time for the leading, the pieces will fit.

If you don't have grozing pliers, or even household pliers, you can use the notches on the cutter. Each notch has a different thickness — use the notch nearest to the thickness of the glass. Gently groze (chew away) a little at a time, being firm but not overbearing.

The edges on your cut glass will be very sharp. Dull the edges of your glass by scraping the edge with a piece of glass, rubbing perpendicular to the other piece. You can also use the carborundum stone. Remember: the edges of the glass are very sharp — try to resist the temptation of feeling the edges with your fingers.

After smoothing out your glass pieces, you're ready to assemble your project. You'll have to decide whether you want to use the leading technique or the copper foil technique.

Leading Technique

Leading is what joins the pieces of glass together. There are two types of leading: a double-channel lead (the H-lead) and the singlechannel lead (the U-lead). The face of the H-lead is either flat or round and is sometimes called the leaf. Flat H-lead is used in modern designs; the round H-lead is used in the traditional designs.

You'll have to choose which kind of lead is appropriate for the type of glass as well as the pattern you're using.

Before using the lead, stretch it so that it becomes more rigid. This makes the lead easier to cut. Keep unused lead wrapped in newspapers or in an old cloth to prevent oxidation. Also, make certain you've cleaned up all excess glass chips and slivers in your work area. Remember — neatness and care can make a difference in the finished appearance of your project.

Lay your pattern (called a cartoon) on the workbench. Position your cut glass pieces on top of the cartoon. Your working pattern will now be on the surface on which you'll be leading. Tape the working pattern to a piece of plywood — don't use nails or tacks — they get in the way.

If your project is in the shape of a square or rectangle, you'll have to make a wooden frame to hold all the pieces together while you're leading. You'll need four wooden lath strips to make the frame. Nail one lath strip along the left-hand side and along the bottom. Use a 90-degree triangle to make sure the lath strips are even. Later, as you lead the glass pieces together, you'll need to frame the other two sides with the remaining two lath strips.

It's better to practice cutting the lead before you cut the pieces for your project. Lead is a soft material, so use care when cutting it. Rock the knife from side to side and cut through the lead gently. Make sure the knife is sharp and the surface on which you're cutting is stable and firm.

Next, use the lathekin to smooth out the lead edges and open the channels so that the glass will fit inside.

Using four strips of lead, make a lead frame inside the wooden frame. This will hold all the glass pieces together after you remove the wooden frame in the end. Make sure the lead frame is perfectly straight, otherwise your glass pieces won't fit right.

The frame is now ready and you may begin laying the pieces of glass out and leading them on the pattern.

Use a small piece of wood and a hammer to gently tap the edge of glass until it is firmly set in the lead.

After the first piece of lead is fitted, make sure the piece of glass falls directly on the cut line of your working pattern. Check the fit of each piece of glass.

Horseshoe nails hold the glass pieces onto your working pattern. Place the horseshoe nails at key pressure points and be sure to remove the nail when you fit the next piece of glass.

Measure the necessary length, and cut the lead about 1/16 of an inch shorter than it measured. This will leave room for the overlay of leaf when you intersect the lead. The lead must join together tightly with no spaces in between. Put the leaded glass back on the working pattern (also known as the cartoon). Hold it in place with a glazing nail and a small scrap piece of lead.

After the first piece of glass is leaded and in place, the next pieces are a little tricky. They will have to lock in place, giving support to one another. Be sure you carefully plan the leading sequence beforehand so your glass project — called a panel — will be secure.

After the last piece is in place, nail the four lath strips in place. This will hold everything in place while you solder. Check to see if the lead joints are smooth and fit snugly and there are no holes.

Soldering is not as complicated as the leading. Actually, it's the fastest and most simple process of stained glass. Try to find an iron that has an iron-clad tip. This is important for effective heat diffusion.

The most difficult part about soldering is keeping a constant temperature. Usually the irons don't come with an on and off switch, but these are found in hardware stores and are easy to attach.

First test the heat of your iron by melting a piece of solder. It should flow easily and constantly. If you see peaks forming, you'll know that the iron isn't hot enough.

Be careful not to leave the iron plugged in when you're not using it. And never clean the iron by immersing it in water.

Now you'll need to clean all the joints in your panel. Use a wire brush and gently rub off the lead oxide and dirt. The solder will flow easier and will create a stronger bond.

Next you must place the oleic acid flux. Flux is used to clean and remove impurities that the wire brush missed. The flux also causes the solder to flow and adhere to the lead. Lightly dab all the joints with the flux — solder will only stick where flux has been applied. After you've soldered, use a rag to remove any excess flux. The longer the flux is left on the panel, the more difficult it is to remove later.

Don't use too much solder — usually 1/8 of an inch is enough. Place the end of the solder over the leaded joint and press down firmly with the flat side of the iron. The solder should flow easily. Lift the solder iron stright up. Do not push the solder around — it may melt the lead or crack the glass. It's a good idea to practice this technique on a scrap of lead first.

The soldered joint should be smooth and flat. This process should only take a few seconds. A poorly soldered joint is pitted and lumpy. This is usually caused by an iron that is too cool, or perhaps no flux was applied.

Now wipe off excess flux with a rag. Check for gaps and loose joints. Most important, check the four outside corners that frame your panel. If everything is intact and soldered, you're ready to turn over the panel.

The panel must be turned with care when only one side has been soldered. The glass is heavy and may cause the unsupported panel to sag.

Remove the lath strips that were framing the panel. Now slide the panel toward you and slowly turn the entire piece over so that the unsoldered side faces up now.

The entire panel is ready for cementing and cleaning. The cement fills any small spaces between the lead and the glass. It's better to do this immediately after you've finished your panel. Cementing strengthens the panel. It also weatherproofs the panel and keeps the glass pieces from rattling.

Use gray metal sash putty to cement the panel. Pinch a small ball of putty between your thumb and forefinger. Force the putty between the lead channel and the glass. Continue this until you've done one side.

Now use the lathekin, or wooden dowel, to flatten the lead down against the glass. The excess putty will ooze out from the lead channel. Keep the glass clean by wiping it off with a soft cloth. Try not to let any of the putty dry on the glass.

Unless your panel is going to be exposed to the outside, it is not necessary to do both sides. It is best, though, to cement both sides for reinforcement.

After you've cemented the panel, you'll need to clean the panel with either plaster of Paris or sawdust. Both of these will absorb the oil from the putty and any flux residue.

Generously apply the plaster over the entire panel. Now scrub it away with a clean bristle brush. You may need to repeat this several times to thoroughly clean your panel.

Now let the panel sit undisturbed for a few days in order for the cement to set. After the cement is completely dry, you may use window cleaner to remove dirt and smudges.

Copper Foil Technique

In many ways, the copper foil technique is easier and less of a mess than the traditional leaded technique. However, this technique can be more time consuming than the leaded stained glass.

Copper foil became popular in the early 1900s because of its flexibility. Copper foil is convenient for small intricate designs, and it is actually stronger than lead came for larger designs.

Before you begin, make sure the glass is clean and free from any dirt or oil. Smooth out the rough edges with a carborundum stone.

When all the edges are cleaned and smoothed out, you're ready to wrap the pieces in the foil. Peel off enough copper to go around the glass piece, plus about 1/4 of an inch for overlapping. Now remove the adhesive backing. Center the glass piece in the foil strip, making sure that there is an even amount of overhang on both sides of the glass. Now mold the strip of copper foil around the glass piece. Press the foil to the edge of the glass piece with your lathekin. Make sure the foil is smooth and tight against the glass.

If there is even a slight difference in the amount of foil hanging over the edge of the glass piece, you'll need to trim away the excess with an X-acto knife.

After all the glass pieces have been wrapped in the foil, position all the pieces on the working board. Hold the pieces in place with lath strips or with push pins.

Now you can apply oleic acid flux to the edges of the foil. Apply just enough solder to join the wrapped pieces securely together. This is known as tack soldering. The purpose of this step is to just hold the pieces together so they won't slip apart when you begin to do the final soldering. You don't have to tack solder both sides with this step.

After the tack soldering is completed and all the pieces are joined, you're ready for the final step of soldering.

Again, apply the flux to exposed areas of the copper foil wrap. While holding the soldering iron over the copper foil, bring the end of the solder wire to the tip of the iron and move them both along the length of the foil seam. Don't worry about gaps between the glass pieces — you can fill these later by filling the space with copper foil.

After you've soldered the entire panel and you've checked for gaps and loose glass pieces, you need to turn the panel over and repeat the final soldering process.

After you've soldered both sides of the panel, you don't need to cement the panel, but you do have to clean away all the excess oleic acid, oil, and dirt. Again, you may either use plaster of Paris or sawdust. Sprinkle the plaster over the panel and scrub with a clean bristle brush. You may need to repeat this step. Brush away leftover plaster. Now you can use window cleaner to get rid of smudges.

You've just completed your stained glass panel. The panel can be mounted onto a wooden frame and installed as a window. You can also make jewelry, trinket boxes, lamps, and many other projects.

Supplies

Here are some places where you'll find everything you need to make your stained glass treasures. Write to them for more information and a catalogue.

For complete stained glass needs:

WHITTEMORE-DURGIN
Box A2065
Hanover, MA 02339
Cost: $1.00 for a catalogue

CORAN-SHOLES
Department H
Box 55
Boston, MA 02127
Cost: $1.00 for a catalogue

For solder at wholesale prices:

SOLDER-CRAFT
P.O. Box 668
Jerico, New York 11763
Call toll free: 800-645-4808

Instructions

Now that you know how to create PVC furniture, you'll need the supplies. Available Plastics, Inc. is a company dedicated to helping you manufacture PVC furniture. Included are their price lists. Be sure to carefully read their shipping and ordering policies to avoid any misunderstandings.

1) All orders must be confirmed in writing. Orders shipped on customer's verbal instructions will be shipped at customer's risk.
2) All orders must be paid for in advance.
3) Orders will be shipped Freight Collect (UPS).
4) No returned goods wil be accepted without written permission by Available Plastics, Inc. There will be a 15 percent restocking charge on all returned goods.
5) Damage during shipping must be settled between the shipper and the customer.
6) Refused goods which cannot be delivered and are returned to API become the property of API. The customer must pay all shipping charges before those goods can be claimed.
7) There will be a $10 surcharge on all orders under $300.

Follow these steps to receive your order quickly:
1) Send a written order using both the catalogue numbers and description, as well as the list price of each item. Add $10 if your order is less than $300.
2) Send a Money Order, Cashiers Check or Certified Check with your order. Personal and company checks are held until the check clears the bank -- usually for 30 days.
3) Be prepared to pay freight fees in cash.
4) Special shipping instructions should be included with each order. Don't forget to put your telephone number on all orders.

There s also a purchase plan on the following page for qualified customers. This plan will enable you to receive discounts on most products, as well as establish credit and eliminate the need for cash-only transactions.

60

Credit Application

Principal Owners or Stockholders
    Name   Address

_____ _____

_____ _____

_____ _____

Company Name   _____

Company Address _____

Telephone # _____ Tax # _____

When Organized _____ Total Net Worth
                                       (approx.) _____

Name of Bank _____ Bank Phone # _____

Trade   _____ Phone # _____
References
          _____   _____

          _____   _____

Are you willing to furnish Company Financial Data? _____

                         Personal Financial Data? _____

Your expected monthly purchases for PVC Furniture Components. $_____

    I understand that this information is given to determine if I qualify for consideration as a special customer of Available Plastics, Inc. and would like more information on the Purchase Plan for Qualified Customers. This request does not obligate me in any way.

                         Signed _____

                         Title   _____

                         Date   _____

CAT. NO.	DESCRIPTION	PRICE
KCC101	Club Chair, curved back with sling	$23.50
KDC102	Dining Chair, with 2 slings* (no cushion required)	22.00
KLS101	Basic Love Seat, with 2 slings	46.00
KCL101	Deluxe Chaise Lounge, with sling	54.00
KSL101	Sunlounge, with sling* (no cushion needed)	35.00
KPB101	Pedastal Base, fits 36", 42", & 48" Tables	12.50
KDK101	Reclining Deck Chair, with sling	36.50

* Solid Colored slings--yellow, green, and blue only

Specify pipe color: White, Beige, or Vanilla only
Sling match color of pipe

All pipe in 1¼" size

UM100	Umbrella (7½' dia.)	65.00
UM100	Umbrella Base	9.00
UF100	Umbrella Frame (7½' dia.)	30.00

CAT NO	DESCRIPTION	PRICE
S100	Sling for Lounge Chairs, Love Seats, Swings & Gliders, seat 17"x27½", back: 18¼"	$ 5.50
*S101	Sling for Club Chair CC101 seat: 16¼" x 26"; back: 18¼"	5.00
*S200	Sling for Dining Chair DC101 seat: 15" x 22 3/8" ; back: 15½"	5.00
S300	Sling for Ottoman OT102 & OT101 11½" x 20"	2.50
S400	Sling for Chaise Lounge CL201 26 3/4" x 81"	18.00
S401	Sling for Chaise Lounge CL102 26½" x 67¼"	15.00
S402	Sling for Chaise Lounge CL101 26½" x 72"	16.00
S500	Sling for Lounge Chair LC205 seat: 19" x 29¼"; back: 20 3/4"	6.50
S501	Sling for Reclining Deck Chair DK101 16½" x 24½"	3.00
S600	Sling for Sun Lounge SL101 28½" x 78"	15.00
*S700	Sling for Dining Chair DC102 (see Note 1) and Bar Stool (set of 1) 11" x 19¼" x 22"; back: 15¼"	4.00
S800	Sling for Bar Stool BS101 9¼" x 16 3/8"	2.00
S900	Sling for Bar Chair BS102 seat: 13" x 22¼"; back: 15"	3.00
S010	Sling for Bar BR102 (see Note 1) 9½" x 49 3/4"	7.50
S011	Sling for Magazine Rack MR001 (see Note 1) 13½" x 27¼"	2.00
S012	Sling for Captain Chair LC107 & LC207 (set of 2) top: 9¼" x 23"; seat: 13¼" x 23¼"	5.00
*S013	Sling for Sun Chair 15¼" x 50½"	5.00
S014	Bag for Catch All CA001 (see Note 1) 15½" Dia. x 21" Long	6.50
S015	Sling (cover) for Swing Canopy SC001 36" x 70"	12.00

Notes:

* These items must be ordered on lots of 4 each.

1 These items are in solid colors only- Blue, Green and Yellow

There is a $2.50 charge of all non-standard slings.

Cushion Shells:

These cushion shells are made with the highest quality vinyl-coated polyester. They are made from one peice of fabric with Delrin zippers in the center for ease of filling and closing. No sewing is necessary. Order by pattern number.

CAT NO	TYPE	SIZE CUSHION	PRICE
C100S	for Lounge Chair, Love Seats, Swings and Gliders	21" x 42"	$12.25
C101S	for Club Chair, CC101	19" x 38"	11.50
C200S	for Dining Chair, DC101	18" x 35"	10.75
C300S	for Ottoman, OT102 & OT101	19" x 19"	5.50
C400S	for Chaise Lounge CL201	22" x 74"	18.00
C401S	for Chaise Lounge CL102 & CL101	22" x 69"	16.50
C500S	for Lounge Chair LC205 & Deck Chair DK101	22" x 47"	14.00
C600S	for Bar Stool BS101	15½" x 15½"	4.50
C700S	for Bar Chair BS102	16" x 33"	9.75

Nylon Buttons: (100/pkg.)

CAT NO	COLOR	PRICE/100
BW001	White	$ 4.50
BB001	Beige	4.75
BV001	Vanilla	4.75
BD001	Dark Brown	4.75

Button Ties: (Polyester)

CAT NO	LENGTH	PRICE/100
BT125	1¼"	$ .90
BT150	1½"	1.00
BT200	2"	1.10

Holofil:

CAT NO	WIDTH	WT. ROLL approx.	$/Lb.	PRICE/ROLL
HL20	20"	8.75	$2.50	$21.88
HL22	22"	9.6	2.50	24.00
HL24	24"	10.5	2.50	26.25

Auxiliary Items:

CAT NO	DESCRIPTION	PRICE
N100	12" needle for buttoning cushions	27.50 ea.
N200	Templates for marking cushion (Designate cushion number)	6.00 ea.
WT100	Polyester White Thread **Approx. 1.1 lbs./sp.**	19.81 sp.
PF02	PVC Coated Fabric	4.90 yd.

CAT NO	DESCRIPTION	PRICE
C100	Cushion for Lounge Chair, Love Seats, Swings and Gliders, 21" x 42"	$20.00
*C101	Cushion for Club Chair 101	19.00
*C200	Cushion for Dining Chair DC101	18.50
C300	Cushion for Ottoman OT102 & OT101	10.00
C400	Cushion for Chaise Lounge CL201	35.50
C401	Cushion for Chaise Lounge CL102 & CL101	34.00
C500	Cushion for Lounge Chair LC205 and Deck Chair DK101	29.00
C600	Cushion for Bar Stool BS101	9.50
C700	Cushion for Bar Chair BS102	18.00

NOTES:

* These items must be ordered in lots of 4 each.

<u>There is an additional charge for non-standard cushions.</u>

$5.00 extra.

CAT NO	DESCRIPTION	QTY	PRICE	PRICE/BOX
1¼":				
125L	1¼" Elbow	125/bx.	.44	$ 55.00
125T	1¼" Tee	100/bx.	.52	52.00
125TL	1¼" Tee-L (slip tee)	150/bx.	.45	67.50
125L3	1¼" 3-Way-L	75/bx.	.69	51.75
125T4	1¼" 4-Way-Tee (side arm tee)	50/bx.	.75	37.50
125X	1¼" Cross	75/bx.	.80	60.00
125C	1¼" Cap (universal)	100/bx.	.27	27.00
125TC	1¼" Table Cap	100/bx.	.29	29.00
1½":				
150L	1½" Elbow	75/bx.	.54	40.50
150T	1½" Tee	50/bx.	.65	32.50
150L3	1½" 3-Way-L	50/bx.	.89	44.50
150X	1½" Cross	50/bx.	.95	47.50
150C	1½" Cap (universal)	300/bx.	.35	105.00
150TC	1½" Table Cap	250/bx.	.37	92.50
BAMBOO FITTINGS:				
125LB	1¼" Elbow, Bamboo	125/bx.	.55	68.75
125TB	1¼" Tee, Bamboo	100/bx.	.65	65.00
COPPER TUBE SIZE:				
75ctsL	3/4" cts. Elbow	100/bag	.21	21.00
75ctsT	3/4" cts. Tee	100/bag	.23	23.00
75ctsC	3/4" cts. Cap	100/bag	.18	18.00
CM	Chaise Mech	150/bx.	.44	66.00

PVC PIPE (case lots only)

CAT NO	DESCRIPTION	QTY	PRICE	PRICE/BOX
35125	1¼" pipe (4' length)	112 ft.	.45	50.40
35125	1¼" pipe (10' length)	100 ft.	.45	45.00
45150	1½" pipe (4' length)	88 ft.	.57	50.16
45150	1½" pipe (10' length)	80 ft.	.57	45.60
75cts	3/4" cts. pipe (5' length)	150 ft.	.25	37.50
65200	2" pipe (10' length)	50 ft.	.87	43.50

PVC CEMENT (single or case lots)

SIZE	PRICE/EACH	NO/CASE	PRICE/EACH
½ pint	$ 1.70	20	$ 32.00
1 pint	2.80	20	53.00
1 quart	3.95	12	55.00
1 gallon	15.50	4	60.50

CAT NO	DESCRIPTION	PRICE
T101	36" x 62" Dining Table Top for CT101	$ 86.00
T102	36" x 36" Dining Table Top for DT102	50.00
T201	24" x 42" Coffee Table Top for CT101	39.00
T301	19" x 24" End Table Top for ET101 & ET102	17.50
T401	16" x 40" Bar Top for BR102	24.75
T402	12" x 23½" Bar Shelf for BR102	11.00
T501	10" x 10" Fern Stand Top for PS101	3.75
T502	One each 10" x 10"; 10" x 8"; 10" x 24" Tops for PS002	16.00
T601	12" x 26" Etagere Shelves (5 each needed for ES101; 4 needed for ES102)	10.50ea
T701	19" x 21" Mobile Server Tray for MS101 (1 or 2 needed)	15.00ea

WERZALIT TOPS

T18WR	18" White round table top	$ 9.40
T18AR	18" Vanilla round table top	10.74
T24WR	24" White round table top	16.75
T24AR	24" Vanilla round table top	18.50
T24WS	24" White square table top	18.50
T24AS	24" Vanilla square table top	20.00
T36WR	36" White round table top	31.70
T36AR	36" Vanilla round table top	34.60
T42WR	42" White round table top	38.70
T42AR	42" Vanilla round table top	42.25
T48WR	48" White round table top	47.50
T48AR	48" Vanilla round table top	55.85
T55WR	55" White round table top	60.25
T55AR	55" Vanilla round table top	64.50
T2442W	24" x 42" White desk top	32.50
T2442A	24" x 42" Vanilla desk top	34.00

NOTE: $2.50 EXTRA CHARGE FOR TOPS WITH AN UMBRELLA HOLE
$1.50 EXTRA CHARGE FOR INSERTS AND PLUGS FOR TABLE TOPS WITHOUT HOLES

Cat #	Description	Price/ea	12 or more

FURNITURE BENDS

BENT BACK FOR CHAIRS - curved back pipe for greater comfort across the shoulders.

FC101	For Lounge Chair LC101	$2.00	$1.50
FC102	For Club Chair CC101	2.00	1.50
FC103	For Dining Chair DC101 & DC102	2.00	1.50
FC104	For Bar Stool and Chair BS102	2.00	1.50

DROP ARMS FOR CHAIRS - curved arm pipe

FC111	For LC101, LS101, LS103, SW101 (set of 2)	4.50/set	3.50/set
FC112	For CC101 (set of 2)	4.50/set	3.50/set

SIDE BEND - curved back for DC102

FC121	Dining Chair DC102 (set of 2)	4.50/set	3.50/set

CHAISE MECHANISM

CM — MOULDED SCALLOPED PLASTIC - can be mounted in 1/2" Sch 40 or 3/4" cts for use with 5 position Chaise Lounge (set of 2) — 1.22/set — 24/box .48/each

FC201 — CHAISE MECHANISM MOUNTED in 3/4" cts pipe (set of 2) — 3.80/set — 3.40/set

FC202 — FC201 Complete with frame to fit Chaise Lounge CL101, CL102 and DK101 — 6.50 — 5.80

CHAISE SIDE JOINTS

FC21 — CHAISE SIDE JOINT - fabricated from one 1 1/2" tee and one 1 1/4" elbow and having 3/4" cts axel capped on each end. Used on CL201 Chaise Lounge. (set of 2) — 6.00/set — 5.40/set

FC212 — CHAISE SIDE JOINT - fabricated from 1 1/4" x 24" pipe flattened on one end, mounted with a 1 1/4" tee and a 3/4" cts axel capped on one end with a coupling on the other end. Pipe has 7/8" hole to accept Chaise Mechanism Frame FC202 used on CL101 Chaise Lounge. (set of 2) — 5.60/set — 5.00/set

GLIDER HANGERS

HANGERS FOR GLIDER - made from 3/4" cts pipe, flattened on ends and drilled with 3/8" holes. (set of 4)

FC301 — For Glider GL101 - 15" between hole centers. — 4.50/set — 4.05/set

FC302 — For Glider GL102 (single seat) 9 1/2" between hole centers. — 4.10/set — 3.70/set

Free Grants & Low-Interest Loans
Lloyd Sanders

Have you ever wondered how people with credit ratings lower than yours obtain money? The only difference between them and you is that they know how and where to get the money. Every year billions of dollars are given to people just like you. Would you like to stake your share? You can, by owning one of the most complete books on money-financing systems. It shows you how to get money from almost every possible source available. Hundreds of methods of raising money are covered in this book.

- Get up to $500,000 in easy-to-qualify SBA loans
- Get up to $350,000 if you're in business and handicapped
- Get up to $315,000 in low-income assistance
- Raise $50,000 with no collateral
- Borrow up to $100,000 from any commercial bank
- Raise up to $50,000,000 the corporate way
- Get up to $67,000 for a home purchase
- Get up to $5,000 a year for education
- Get up to $92,000 for home improvements
- Get up to $150,000 if you are a woman in business
- Learn loopholes in bank policies
- Use creative financing to raise large amounts of capital
- Use advanced banking techniques to get loans
- 270 foundations that will give you a free grant
- Get some of the $3 billion given out by foundations every year
- Get money from 300 financial institutions that loan by mail

These are just some of the money-raising techniques included. *Free Grants & Low-Interest Loans* must contain almost every known method of raising money. Each 5½-by-8½-inch book is $7.

How To Use Your Hidden Potential To Get Rich
David Bendah

This book presents a program that clearly maps the route self-made millionaires took to make their fortunes. Any very successful person who has made millions has used the techniques in this book.

Hidden Potential will show any individual, regardless of skill, intelligence and experience, how to use the mind to realize both business and personal dreams.

A complete success program, it is illustrated with charts and diagrams that enable understanding of the mind-transformation process. Included are quizzes that monitor the reader's progress to wealth. David Bendah, the author, backs up his points with interesting examples of how ordinary people—from Milton Hershey to William Colgate—used the same techniques to make fortunes. Bendah also devotes three chapters to Japanese wealth-building techniques. In short, this volume is designed to expose the reader to every success principle needed to get rich.

$200,000 In 24 Hours & 130 Other Moneymaking Reports

#0333   Did you ever wonder what companies give you when they offer to make you an instant millionaire overnight? When they offer you instant credit regardless of your past? Well, now for the first time, almost every moneymaking plan and idea on the market has been compiled into one package with reproduction rights, so you can reproduce all or some of these reports. Here are some of the reports you will receive:

- Raise $200,000 in 24 hours without collateral
- Turn bad credit ratings into AAA-1 credit ratings
- Win oil & gas leases in gov't held public drawings
- Profit from a large list of valuable tax loopholes
- Wipe Out all your debts fast without bankruptcy
- Get Rich in mail order, many complete programs
- Stop Paying property taxes! Forever, legally
- Free Subscriptions To More Than 100 Magazines
- Borrow $50,000,000 on your signature for any purpose
- Get Free car, food, clothing, furniture, rent...
- Produce cheap, whiskey, rum, gin, vodka & other liquors
- Convert Your TV into a movie-size screen TV
- Get auto fuel for 15 cents a gallon or produce gasohol
- Purchase a new car for Only $50 above dealer's cost
- Get a $1,000,000 life insurance policy with no cash
- Get an expensive mansion Without Cost
- Get Free Canadian land • Free oil for your car
- Take over a going business with Zero Cash
- Get 300% more on your savings account
- Get gov't land $2.25 an acre • Free Airline Travel
- Strike It Rich with gov't assistance (minerals)
- Own a $1,000,000 corporation in 4 weeks for Only $50
- Buy Gov't Surplus 2 cents on the dollar
- Buy valuable apt., homes & land for next to nothing
- Get All The Credit Cards you will ever want

This is only a small fraction of the reports included. Your kit includes more than 130 full-length reports with reproduction rights.

999 Little-Known Businesses That Can Make You A Fortune
William Carruthers

#2155   This book is a collection of 999 businesses that have made their owners rich. It shows you how hundreds of your ordinary talents can be converted into cash and your own business. The majority of ideas require little or no capital and can be started in your spare time. It gives you such a large variety of projects to undertake that you are sure to find that perfect moneymaker for you. Each plan has been carefully selected as a little-known, unfamiliar business that is completely overlooked in most areas of this country. Each is free of competition and has a personality all its own. Use this book to create that special business that will make you financially independent. This book is 5-by-8-inches and has 258 pages.

$2,000 An Hour

David Bendah

Would you like $2,000 for just making a few phone calls and looking in a few directories? That is all you have to do to enjoy this kind of money. If you can read English and can talk on the phone, you will be able to make thousands of dollars in a few hours.

One out of 10 Americans owns unclaimed property worth $325 billion. This amount increases by $1 billion every year. These poeple have forgotten or lost their money in bank accounts, stocks and unclaimed insurance policies. The states make no real effort to contact these money owners. Why should they, when unclaimed property is one of their biggest sources of revenue, second only to taxes?

As soon as you receive this book, you could make up to $2,000 an hour. All you need is a phone and a telephone book. This proven ingenious system in this book can be learned in one half hour. After that, you are all set. If you can read English and can talk on the phone, you could be making $2,000 an hour.

Get Rich With No Work

David Holmes & Joel Andrews

You can get rich without working by using the multi-level approach. Let me explain it. Your agents get the product from the company, but you get the commission from your agents and each agent they enlist. Others do the work while you sit back and collect the high commissions. Thousands of people just like you are making more than $100,000 a year without working. Once you have this book you can begin to create your fortune with any product you choose.

Holmes and Andrews, the authors, have a combined 20 years of sales and marketing experience. Holmes, a marketing expert and author of two books, has made more than 150 television and radio appearances over the past year. Andrews, who has personally launched six successful business ventures, is so highly regarded in sales and marketing that he has testified on marketing to both Houses of Congress. Together, these men teach you how to get rich without working.

Making $500,000 A Year In Mail Order
David Bendah

If you ever dreamed of having your mailbox crammed with thousands of envelopes each containing a check in your name, working any hours you want, whenever you want, and being able to afford the pleasures life has to offer in one of this country's most lucrative businesses, then this book can make those dreams a reality.

Many people, including the author, have made a lot of money in mail order. Mail order is one of the most lucrative businesses you can get involved in. Work in your home, part-time if you want, to realize your life-long dreams of security.

Bendah's book is full of helpful, easy-to-understand information. Bendah, considered one of the nation's leading ad writers, teaches laymen how best to use his unique techniques and explains every aspect of book formation and marketing. He even goes so far as to print his confidential ad results from the many successful mail order ads he has run. He discloses his secret formula that has ensured the success of many mail order businesses. If you ever had a dream of making it big in mail order, *Making $500,000 A Year In Mail Order* can be your key.

Make A Fortune & Travel Absolutely Free!
Ben & Nancy Dominitz

Have you heard about the fat commission checks and free travel benefits in the travel business? This book reveals how you can do both without using a dime of your own money. This book shows you how to:
- Start your travel business out of your home in your spare time
- Add a minimum of 50% to your present income
- Travel free, a guest of air and cruise lines and tour companies
- Receive a discount on all airline tickets and hotel bills
- Make a fortune with group travel and much, much more

Use this book to start a new profitable business or just to save money on all your travels. Get this complete hard-bound, 209-page, 9½-by-6½-inch guide for only $20.

$10,000 A Month Making PVC Furniture

Sam Glassman

There is big money to be made in PVC furniture. All you need to make beautiful, profit-making furniture is a hacksaw, pencil, tape measure, glue and some of your spare time. Here is what is included in your book:
- Where you can buy PVC pipe wholesale
- Detailed, easy-to-follow plans of the hottest-selling furniture
- A complete marketing plan that will show you how to sell your furniture to anxious buyers
- How to make up to $100 an hour with these easy-to-assemble furniture pieces.
- Photographs and step-by-step instructions

The craze is on. PVC furniture that never needs painting is commanding high prices at your local furniture stores. Not only are people buying this non-corroding, sturdy furniture for outdoors, but interior designers are recommending its use indoors. You can make a lot of money in this hot new business with this complete guide to PVC furniture.

Operating A High-Profit Financial Brokerage Business

Jason Hunter

This book is certainly the largest single volume Financial Broker course you can buy. It's 8½ x 11 and 260 pages long. This book will teach you how to acquire money from 2,500 different sources. It includes complete forms and detailed instruction. The foolproof methods in this book will guarantee you will get the loan of your choice. Here are the type of loan sources listed.

- Mortgage Companies
- Venture Capital
- SBIC's
- Mideast & N. African Banks
- Trusts
- Invention & Idea Finance
- Construction companies
- Pension Funds
- Private Funding Corp.
- Agricultural Loans
- Economic Opportunity
- Real Estate Investment
- Business & Executive Loans
- Foundations
- Commercial Banks
- Savings & Loan Assoc.
- Leasing Companies
- Insurance Companies
- Underwriting Firms
- Factoring
- Savings Banks
- SBA Loans
- Educational Loans
- International Loans
- Finance Companies
- Government Loans

With your directory you can choose from thousands of active sources for all of your money needs. Order your copy today.

The Self-Publisher's Opportunity Kit

#1633

The Self-Publisher's Opportunity Kit contains eight interesting books—they've all been tested and are proven sellers. Each book comes with a copyright agreement, which allows you to reprint and sell as many copies as you wish, and complete, step-by-step instructions on how to market these books for the greatest profit.

In addition to the eight titles, you get proven-effective classified ads and a sales letter to promote your books. Some of the books measure 24, 8½-by-11-inch pages.

The eight books are:
1. How To Get Free Grants
2. Importing—Your Key To Success
3. Making A Fortune With Real Estate
5. The Secret Of Raising Money
6. The Millionaire's Secret Of Growing Rich
7. How To Influence People And Win Them Over
8. How To Get $200,000 In Benefits From The U.S. Gov't

The Self-Publisher's Opportunity Kit, with eight books, certificate of reprint rights, step-by-step instructions, sales letter and classified ads, is only $30.

How To Write A Good Advertisement
Victor Schwab

#1455

The more books on advertising you study, the better you will be at writing ads. One book I especially recommend is *How To Write A Good Advertisement, A Short Course In Copywriting*, by Victor O. Schwab, one of the best copywriters of this century. He created many famous ads—one, for *How To Win Friends And Influence People*, sold 5 million copies for author Dale Carnegie.

Schwab's techniques are continuously studied by the top advertising agencies, and you should study them, too. Instead of focusing on the structure of the successful ad, Schwab concentrates on the psychology of the consumer. If you know what consumers want and need, your ads will do very well. After reading this book, you should be able to pinpoint the precise needs of your customers and know how to fulfill them. This 227-page, 8½-by-11-inch detailed book can be yours for only $16.

Home Business Opportunities

Russ von Hoelscher

Small business/home business authority Russ von Hoelscher offers you scores of new, dynamic, unusual and proven ways to make lots of money in the comfort of your own home. In addition to almost 100 home business moneymaking plans (most of which can be started with little or no investment), there are in-depth sections on making money in mail order and how to prosper as an information-age "how-to" author and/or publisher.

Take advantage of this volume so that you can make money at home. This informative, 365-page book lets you stay home and be a moneymaking success.

Building A Mail Order Business

William Cohen

Another book I recommend highly is *Building A Mail Order Business, A Complete Manual For Success*, by William Cohen. This book is hard bound and 495 pages. It covers every aspect of selling by mail, from the basics to the most sophisticated techniques for increasing sales. Every method is explained in a detailed, logical fashion that shows you, step-by-step, how to do it and do it right. This is one of the most complete up-to-date guides on mail order. Cohen covers product selection, writing, graphics, competition and the legal aspects of mail order. This complete mail order manual is available for only $20.